Haynes

Drum-Kit
Manual

Haynes Publishing

**For Bill Balmer, George Balmer, my sons
Jon and Karl and my nephew Peter**

'The drumming gene marches on'

First published in February 2012

A catalogue record for this book is available from the British Library

ISBN 978 0 85733 097 0

Library of Congress catalog card no. 2011935261

Published by Haynes Publishing,
Sparkford, Yeovil, Somerset BA22 7JJ, UK

Tel: 01963 442030 Fax: 01963 440001
Int. tel: +44 1963 442030 Int. fax: +44 1963 440001
E-mail: sales@haynes.co.uk
Website: www.haynes.co.uk

Haynes North America, Inc.,
861 Lawrence Drive, Newbury Park,
California 91320, USA

Printed in the USA by Odcombe Press LP,
1299 Bridgestone Parkway, La Vergne, TN 37086

Haynes

Drum-Kit
Manual
How to buy, maintain and
improve your drum-kit

Paul Balmer

Contents

Foreword Steve Gadd

I started drumming aged three, playing along with records of John Philip Sousa marches – playing on a piece of wood with some drumsticks my uncle gave me. Then, at six or seven, I had a little snare, the next year a bass drum arrived as a present and then a hi-hat – I built it up slowly as I went along. Maybe that's a good idea – I don't know!

In 1957, I got my first proper kit, a four-piece Gretsch, and I still have it! It needs some work, but it's a great kit. They had internal mufflers on all those drums, but I couldn't get the right sound until I saw a drummer with trombonist Kay Winding's band, and he had some material stretched against the bass drum head, and that worked.

In those days, I used to do a 10-minute set-up for the whole kit, but now you need two guys to carry one case – everything has changed. The PA guy, the monitor guy and the tech all work together to get a sound – it's a lot different from playing acoustically.

For me, drum kit 'tuning' it's not about a 'note', it's getting a drum to sound good in a certain room – it's trial and error. There are certain things – the fundamentals – that can help; for instance an ambassador coated on top and a clear bottom head gives the drum a little more resonance. I also recommend that you tighten plastic heads as hard as a rock to stretch them, and go down with the top head till it feels comfortable to play, then do the same with the bottom head. Go for a tone that works and gets the drum responding the most that it can. Then add some tape or tissue, Moongel or whatever, to take away the less pleasant overtones. When a drum sounds good by itself, then you have to tune again, so it sounds good going from one drum to the other, so they are not all the same pitch.

It's a combination – the bass drum might be dead on its own, but the toms may be resonating. Then you put the snare drum on and see how much the snares are rattling – and it's different for every room! You go to another space and you have to start all over again!

When I need them, my drums are ready. I'm fortunate now to have techs like Yard Gavrilovic and Scott Hoffman to keep everything up to spec and performing at its best. It wasn't always so, and I did my share of head changes and hardware maintenance in the days when neither were as good as they are now. But it always paid off to look after my gear, and the reward is having time to focus on the real task of serving the song and the singer.

As you will see in the case study of my own kit, I make

notes of important grooves and keep a TAMA Rhythm Watch handy so tempos are always steady – it triggers the memory it reminds you – the arrangements change, but at least you have a point of reference. It's good when I have to count off the band.

When I laid down that now well-known groove for Paul Simon's *50 Ways* at A&R on 48th street, it was simply that day's creative challenge. I'd been toying around with different hi-hats, with the left hand, and the colour of the rudimentary snare drum just seemed right, coupled with syncopation and that great Gretsch bass drum.

Every situation has its different challenges – there are all kinds of ways to make music. You can use notes, but you can also use silence, and that is just as important as what you play. It's challenging to be able to use space and still be able to keep the thing feeling good. Being a musician is about many things, but in the end it's all about listening.

Steve Gadd,
Spring 2012

Foreword Chad Smith

Looking at all the great and very cool drum kits in this book, it struck me that our instrument hasn't changed a great deal since Gene Krupa's days. Sure, some big advances in hardware and shell construction have been made in the last eighty or so years, but the kit I play now with the Chili Peppers or with Chickenfoot is not very different from the one Mr. Krupa played in the 1930s. There's a reason for that: you don't fix it if it ain't broke! The simplest set up of a snare drum, a bass drum, a couple of toms, and some cymbals is still the weapon of choice for most drummers, and in my opinion, it's still the best way to get the point across. The drum kit endures because of this simplicity, but also because it is an incredibly adaptable instrument. Whether it's Max Roach with Charlie Parker, Ringo with The Beatles, Neil Peart with Rush, or some kid with headphones rocking out in his basement, the drum kit is the blank canvas onto which we get to paint our next masterpiece.

I've been really fortunate in my career to have the opportunity to play a lot of different drum kits, and I'm not going to lie to you, it's been pretty awesome. Sitting behind my own kit on a big stage and getting to share my music with a stadium full of people is a dream come true for me. My drums are an extension of me – I communicate my personality, through them.

Over the years I've been lucky enough to see many great drummers play and I've learned something very important; every drummer has his or her own sound and feel they carry with them wherever they go. It's the way they hit the drums and where they put the beat that identifies the drummer. But, the drum kit is the vehicle that makes our identity come alive. It's the instrument that let's the world know who we are.

Chad Smith,
Spring 2012

Introduction

The 'drum kit', or in the USA 'drum set', is an art deco masterpiece straight out of Fritz Lang's classic film *Metropolis*; almost as if some futuristic official had conducted a time and motion study and decided one man could do the work of three. Fortunately one man *can* anchor a groove more convincingly than three!

At the beginning of the 20th or 'jazz century', popular music had inherited two related percussion traditions. The first derived from the Viennese symphonic orchestra with its 'percussion section', two or three skilled individuals working as a team – a bass drum specialist who might also provide the clash of two 'marching cymbals', a snare drum virtuoso who could provide a *ppp* dramatic underpin or *FFF* march to the scaffold, and possibly a timpanist, evoking tuned pomp and thunder. All were capable of doubling on a hundred 'toys', adding triangle and wind machine, whistle and 'bark'. These percussion sections transferred to the music hall and Vaudeville circuits and had a brief moment of glory in the 'not so silent' film era, adding live soundtracks to the silver screen's blank audio canvas.

The other tradition derived from New Orleans, where a similar percussion section played for the syncopated marching bands that inherited their instruments from the American Civil War. In that same city's 'Congo Square' a distinct African tradition also featured percussion sections in which the sons of slaves played calabashes and hand drums. As these evolving 'jass' bands started to 'rest a while and sip' in the bordellos and 'sporting houses', the snare drummer found he could kick the bass drum for an accent and crash a cymbal with a hand-held stick, and in this way the drummer became a one-man powerhouse of rhythm. As a bonus the 'swing' improved – it's a darned sight easier for one guy to push the beat or lean on the backbeat than it is for three.

My first kit was exactly like this. In the 1950s, as a rhythm-crazy schoolboy I joined the Boy Scouts – because they had drums! – and soon invented my own kit. I took their military rope-tensioned bass drum, a rope tensioned 20in snare with the snares removed for a tom, and a brass military side-drum for a snare. The clashed cymbals balanced on an ashtray stand for a ride and I was off – it sounded great! I'm sure 'inventing' this drum kit helped me understand the refinements that came with proprietary kits – and those calf heads sounded so rich.

Back in the early 1900s, with growing horn sections and increased pressure on orchestral pit space, refinement of the 'kicked drum' came with W.F. Ludwig's patented bass-drum pedal of 1909. Soon every manufacturer followed suit. In the early 1920s came the 'low boy', a 10cm high 'lo-hat', and in 1928 the Leedy foot-sock 'hi-hat'.

These genius inventions contributed to the temple-block bejewelled 'contraption kits' ('traps') of the 1920s and '30s and were used to great effect by Warren 'Baby' Dodds on New

ABOVE A bass drum pedal of the 1940s

RIGHT An early 20th century bass drum pedal

BELOW A current DW 'jazz' kit

Orleans showboats, and 'Chick' Webb in New York dancehalls. These revolutions travelled slowly in a pre-aviation, pre-Internet world, and in Liverpool my father Bill Balmer still played a traps kit in the 1940s. Bill was very proud of his furniture-castor Premier traps, which would easily manoeuvre on and off trams – then a common means of transport to gigs. As in most traps kits, the toms originated in China, my father retrieving his literally from a Shanghai steamer in the dock. These were rivet-headed, calf-skinned and crudely 'tuned' by the heat of a fire. The Slingerland Banjo and Drum Company would soon develop 'tunable' toms, adapting the mechanics of their own snare lugs.

Cymbals still came from Turkey, and the alchemic mysteries of Kerop Zildjian were coveted and expensive. Cheaper Western European imitations tended to sound trashy and were never 80/20 bronze.

The modern drum kit revolution reached its climax with Gene Krupa's Slingerland 'Stripped Down' and eventually 'Radio King' outfit of circa 1935. The sight of this sexy kit in the Benny Goodman Orchestra and later in *The Benny Goodman Story* biopic sent a message around the world – one man could drive the biggest band, and solo as well!

Krupa had commissioned this 'tunable tom' four-piece kit himself, and its genius proportions, hi-hat, 'crash' and 'ride' have become the basis of virtually every kit since. From then on the drum kit stopped being a ragtag collection of diverse and historic parts and became recognised as a visual and audio whole. Krupa became the first drummer to record bass drum and toms as well – previously

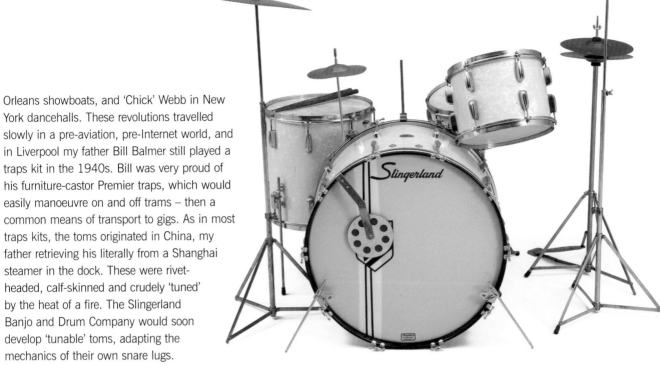

ABOVE A 'Radio King' Slingerland. The fun started here

BELOW Bill Balmer in 1945

engineers had insisted on just snare and cymbals. Seen on film, Krupa still occasionally held his hi-hat in the earlier stopped cymbal style – my dad did this too, with a penny under the cymbal as a bottom 'click'.

This simple modern kit has since provided the groove for everything from *Jailhouse Rock* to *Kind of Blue*, and every great pop song from the Beatles to Broadway. It has often been extended for showpiece solos from players as diverse as Louis Bellson, Buddy Rich, Ginger Baker, Keith Moon and Vinny Appice. Toms have gone from two to twenty-two, and cymbals from one to thirty! But if you need a solid anchor for the pulse, then drummers' trust in the example of Steve Gadd and realise that less is often more!

Whatever the size of the kit or the grandeur of the gig, all drums are intensely mechanical, from tension lugs to hi-hat spring; everything must function in well-lubricated silent service of the intended groove – and do that 10,000 times per night, 300 gigs per year, with potential for a lot of pace-inhibiting friction. Cymbals need to be suspended with freedom and precision, and heads prepared to take an unmerciful pounding.

So if you're starting out let me help you choose a first kit. If you already have a kit, then briefly put down the sticks and brushes and take up a humble spanner – tightening up that rhythm section starts back in the garage!

Remember, every band needs three musicians and an alchemist – you *are* 'The Sultan of Swing'.

Paul Balmer
February 2012

ELECTRIC GUITAR MANUAL

Buying a drum-kit

This is a great time to buy a drum-kit. CNC machining has ensured that even the most modest kit is accurately cut and the components tend to fit. Drum heads have improved dramatically as the space-age science of plastics constantly evolves.

Even budget cymbals can sound OK, and if you have the money, the choice at the top end of the market is fantastic. Hardware has never been more stable and efficient. So enjoy the groove!

LEFT A DW kit with Matt Nolan and Istanbul cymbals.

RIGHT Great hardware.

Buying a first kit and moving up

In the 21st century it's no
longer necessary to spend
a fortune to get started with
a decent-sounding first kit.

The bad old days

In the mid-20th century, with rock'n'roll in its infancy
and jazz still consolidating, the gap between beginners'
kits and pro kits was immense. My first 'Stratford' kit
cost £12, and Rory Storm's drummer Ringo Starr started
with a bass drum that cost £1 10s. Both these early set-ups
were flimsy and sounded weak. Ringo's 'Beatles' Black Oyster
pearl 1963 Downbeat kit would have cost 262 guineas
(without cymbals), and the Premier kits we both had
in the interim approximately £150. Though both these kits could
hold their own today, beginners' options have improved dramatically.

ABOVE A 1964 'Downbeat'.

The present

At the start of the 21st century CNC manufacturing processes and
advances in head technology mean that a well set up economy kit
can now sound and look fine, especially if a little care is taken over
the important details of set-up and attuning.

Most of the major manufacturers now offer entry-level kits as
a complete self-contained package, and these provide amazing
value for money. Cost savings are achieved in the areas of less
expensive timber, less rugged fittings and generally flimsier stands
and hardware. These savings make perfect sense,
as you're unlikely to expect a first kit to endure
the ravages of a world tour.

Another major saving is assembly. Many
beginner kits are now supplied as compact
unassembled parts – shells, heads and
lugs, nuts and bolts and a set of instructions.
I actually see this as a plus, as the beginner can
get a real sense of what drums are and how they
function through the assembly process.

If you're serious about drumming then it's
also worth considering buying some really good
second-hand drums. These can be improved
with good heads, and the money saved used
to buy serious professional stands and fittings.
You can retain this hardware for years, just
upgrading the drums themselves when
finances permit. See page 16 for more on
second-hand options.

LEFT A good
beginners' kit.

Moving up

In the case studies starting on page 112 I've included a range of kits covering most of the key manufacturers. By the time you buy your first pro kit you'll have been playing a while and will know the weaknesses and strengths of the many options available. The range of drum sizes obtainable today reflects the range of music being performed. Huge stadium size toms arranged in sets of six are brilliant for Wembley Arena but not so useful for a little jazz on a pub stage the size of a postage stamp. Equally, a compact kit that records well is the session man's delight but can look out of scale centre-stage at Candlestick Park – it's a case of horses for courses.

A useful first gigging kit.

Choice of woods

Drummers once gave little thought to choice of timber and drum construction; we bought kits because they sounded good and that was it. However, the microscope of the recording studio has revealed significant differences in timber sounds and encouraged more consideration.

Though solid wood drums were common in the early part of the 20th century most modern drums are constructed from some kind of resilient ply. Plywood was developed to promote an ideal combination of light weight and strength, but the number, material, grain orientation and thickness of the constituent ply layers vary immensely from manufacturer to manufacturer. It's now recognised that even the type and thickness of the glue that binds the ply can significantly alter the resonance of a given shell.

Current consensus is that maple ply shells offer a fine grain with a smooth even texture, tending to long, slow sustain and a warm and resonant tone. By contrast birch is a straight-grained wood with a finer texture; known for strength and resilience, this tends to produce a short, fast acoustic response, emphasising the higher harmonics and greater attack.

Some manufacturers combine maple and birch in the same ply, thus potentially offering the best characteristics of both. Some drummers favour maple for a bass drum and birch for toms, others prefer consistent maple or birch construction.

Drums are also manufactured from other woods. African mahogany is a relatively 'soft' hardwood that can offer a dramatic boost in lower frequencies. This bass boost effect is attributed to its loosely packed cellulose network, which creates a Helmholtz resonator-like tuned response in the lower frequencies. Basswood is also common, especially in

economy kits. As pressures on diminishing timber resources increase, manufacturers are constantly experimenting with alternative sources and types of wood.

Furthermore, every individual piece of timber has its own unique character depending on the growing conditions and climate that prevailed whilst the source tree was growing. This means that we can only generalise about timber signature and must in the final analysis judge each drum on its merits and intended purpose.

Sometimes makers add wooden reinforcing hoops to the basic shell for extra strength, definition and focus. These rings vary in size in scale with the drum.

Above all we must consider the kit as a whole and find component drums that work as one internally complementary instrument that suits our individual style of playing.

Hardware

For a first gigging kit I suggest that you buy the best hardware you can possibly afford and keep this even as your drums change. Hardware lets you down more frequently than drums, and a good early investment can save you a lot of cash and time in the long term. (See page 51 for more detailed specifics.)

Cymbals

The same applies to that most personal choice, cymbals – buy with care and think of building complementary matched sets. New is not always better. In fact older cymbals are prized and will often sound a lot better than shiny new economy sets. Seek a sound that inspires you to play more. See page 60 for much more detailed advice on cymbals.

The classic four-shell set-up

This is the set-up that has driven
a million hits, from the cool jazz
of Miles Davis to the creative pop
of the Beatles and all points between.

1 Stand-mounted cymbals
Cymbals were originally
mounted 'birdcage' fashion from
above and were only for dramatic
crashes, but with the trend for 'riding
the cymbal' (with a penny under the
rim for hi-hat-like effects) the steadier
mount from below evolved, initially
clamped precariously to the bass-drum
hoop. Flush-based floor stands have
now given way to much heavier triple-
braced heavy engineering with boom
arms aiding precise placement.

Gene Krupa

Gene Krupa established the
four-drum set-up with two
toms* in 1936, and this
kit became the standard
throughout the 1940s, '50s
and '60s. Then in the 1970s
an additional bass-drum-
mounted 'rack' tom became
common, while today there's
a retro trend back to just
two toms.

* Though for showpiece *Sing
Sing Sing* Gene often liked the
tonal variety offered by two
floor-toms, including an 18in.

Tom toms

2 Krupa liked a 9in x 13in and 16in x 16in and was the first to ask for attuned resonant heads – previously these had been permanently tensioned and brass-tacked 'Chinese' style. The first contraption kit toms were imported from China and were initially considered a novelty item for accompanying 'exotic dancers', but Gene and his hero 'Chick' Webb realised the bigger potential for dramatic fills and intros across the whole set. The 'Krupa' sizes are still a mainstay, but larger and smaller options are widely available.

The snare

3 Borrowed from the battlefield, this small drum once transmitted command signals to troops, its rattling snare cutting through the noise of cannon and muskets. It now drives the backbeat through a wall of guitars, keyboards and brass. Sizes vary, but 6in x 14in is the benchmark, and wood and metal shells vie for popularity. Once catgut, most modern snares are now sprung wire.

Hi-hat

4 Evolved from the marching band 'clashed pair' cymbals of New Orleans, the hi-hat was initially the snowshoe or 'low boy' firmly planted on the ground. Barney Walberg of Walberg and Auge was probably the daring innovator who saw the potential for an extension tube giving a versatile ride and 'chick'.

Bass drum

5 Also borrowed from the military but reduced in height and extended in depth, getting higher in pitch and shorter on sustain. Back now to 'two' heads, batter and resonant, after a '70s trend for single-head 'click', 22in x 18in is a guide size. Krupa's bass drum was originally a 26in, but jazz players go smaller and rock drummers often go bigger. Ludwig standardised the foot-operated bass drum pedal in 1909 and currently double pedals are enjoying popularity.

Second-hand and vintage options

Barring abuse there's not much you can do to permanently damage a drum, so it's worth looking for good-quality classic kits – but NOT odd drums, as other than rare and collectable snares these are less useful and unlikely to blend into a homogenous kit.

ABOVE This 1960s Premier is still being gigged.

The great custom drum-maker Eddie Ryan tells me that older shells were often better made than inexpensive new ones, as quality wood was in plentiful supply until very recently. Old shells with distressed or warped wraps can be refinished or re-covered – perhaps in a rare or custom finish. Old lugs can often be re-chromed and threads replaced.

However, professional repairs aren't cheap, so look for a well cared-for kit if cost is a major factor.

'Bubble' in this '70s wrap.

Chrome starting to pit.

Things to watch out for

■ Damaged bearing edges aren't easy to accurately resurface, so always remove the heads and check for dents and pits, which can make attuning a nightmare.

■ Beware crossed threads and missing bolts in shell lugs – these can't always be replaced with exact replicas, especially on vintage drums.

■ Badly warped hoops are difficult to accurately re-true, and some chrome may be shed in the process.

■ Split or 'out of round' shells are likely to be more trouble than they're worth. This shell has an erroneous manufacturing overlap.

■ Always preserve old badges, as they're highly prized and difficult to accurately replicate. Often these are date specific, which helps with valuations.

■ Unusual snare mechanisms are collectable but can be impractical for regular use if parts are scarce. These rare '60s snare sets have to be custom-made.

■ Old hardware is often strained 'out of true', which makes for slow set ups. Damaged threads here can result in onstage nightmares – this stand will no longer tighten properly. So always assemble a stand in the shop and see if it really does the job.

■ Squeaky pedals may just need lubrication but can often have badly worn bearings and alignment issues. Springs may not be current standard sizes.

■ Hi-hats take a lot of punishment and are worth purchasing new. The internals are fiddly to access and worn parts are often unique.

■ A new set of heads can transform the sound of an old kit; but beware – many pre-1970s shells were non-standard sizes! In the pre-plastic era calfskin heads were individually lapped on the drummer's own hoops, and even some mid-'60s drums were pre-international sizes – as in the picture right. A range of pre-international heads are available from Remo, but the options are very limited.

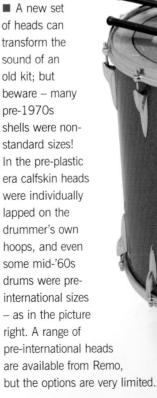

Choosing a snare drum

The sound of a snare drum is every drummers' most personal decision, as the snare is probably the drum that most clearly defines your style and your approach to the kit.

Many serious players are wedded to a particular model for life and will use that same snare as every other part of a set-up changes – think Steve Gadd with his Yamaha 9000, Buddy Rich with his Slingerland Radio King or Keith Moon with his Ludwig Supra-phonic quietly lurking behind a mound of Premier.

Every drummer seems to harbour a dream of a rare pre-war Ludwig 'Black Beauty' only brought out for recordings. There's also a recent cult of 'signature' snares, so the sound of your favourite celebrity player may again play a part.

In choosing your snare it may be helpful to consider the following factors, and assess these against the music you're most frequently asked to play:

Wood or metal?
With roots in military mayhem and the era before miked-up kits, the metal snare with its aggressive high harmonics offered a solution to getting the backbeat heard in almost any situation. The downside for some ears, however, was a lack of 'warmth' – wooden snares certainly offer more low mid-frequencies.

Size matters

My first snare was 14in deep and had a wonderfully resonant sound. It was useless, however, for cutting through the electric guitars of '60s rock'n'roll. Many drummers of this era favoured a shallow, bright snare, now sometimes referred to as a piccolo (though a true piccolo would be less than 14in width). Custom-maker Eddie Ryan makes a brilliant tribute snare based on the drums he made for rock'n'roll pioneer Tony Meehan.

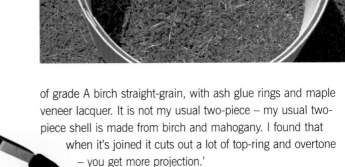

of grade A birch straight-grain, with ash glue rings and maple veneer lacquer. It is not my usual two-piece – my usual two-piece shell is made from birch and mahogany. I found that when it's joined it cuts out a lot of top-ring and overtone – you get more projection.'

The sharp crack of the piccolo is now a favourite second snare for many stadium bands. The particular drum shown here is hand-made and features a Remo Fiberskyn 3 head, reaching for the sound of calfskin vellum. It also has Eddie's signature square lugs and a substantial period-correct internal damper. This is the ideal drum for crisp 'rockabilly' intros.

Eddie told me: 'The snare drum is constructed

A deeper-style snare was repopularised by Led Zeppelin's John Bonham, and miked-up for rock arenas combines the depth of the bigger shell with the penetrating audibility of the classic compromise 5–6in drum. The large shell drum depicted is custom-made by Liberty and features a 14in x 10in shell in white gloss finish, with a nine-ply birch core and multi-length tension rods in a staggered formation. The unusual black 'weave' head is an Evans Onyx.

Hoops

My first snare had wooden hoops and a distinctive voice, especially on rimshots. Snares are most often available now with steel hoops in two main styles: triple-flanged pressed steel for a light open sound – think Ludwig and Pearl; or cast metal for a cutting bright tone – think Gretsch and Premier.

A recent trend has re-presented wooden hoops, which offer a different tone colour – perhaps most suitable for 'unplugged' and acoustic sets.

Specific materials

Metal snares can be brass or steel, and these offer different timbres. Wooden snares were once solid maple as this vintage Slingerland, but are now usually ply. The number of plies varies, and birch, mahogany and maple as well as numerous exotic hardwoods are all available. The general consensus of the qualities of the various materials used is:

- Birch – bright and balanced across the audio spectrum.
- Maple – more emphasis on low frequencies.
- Mahogany – even more low frequencies (on true mahogany, not Philippine).
- Hybrids – offer the best of all worlds.
- Bamboo – eco-friendly and 'tuned' by Drum Workshop.
- Bubinga – 53% harder than maple and birch; acoustically-speaking, Bubinga provides a very sharp and aggressive attack, often tempered in manufacture to broaden its range.
- Acrylics – offer a radical alternative with a range of sounds all their own

But beware of these generalities, particularly concerning wood types, as the moisture content of any piece of wood, its growing conditions and the adhesive used in forming the ply will all contribute to an individual sound to every individual drum – find one you like – and keep it!

Bearing edges

These need to be consistent and free of flaws – a flaw will cause inconsistency in rod tension and present more difficulty in getting an even tension on

the heads. Generally, sharper-angled bearing edges result in less contact with the head and a brighter tone with more high-order harmonics. Pearl, some say, tend to sound 'brighter' than Gretsch – form your own opinion and discuss for at least 50 years...

The drum depicted is again from custom-maker Liberty and features retro tube-lugs and a special pierced Evans head, vented for a quicker response. The 'side stick' sound from the wooden hoop is fabulous.

Snare mechanisms

■ **Conventional strainers** – do the job and are primitive but effective, usually depending on a piece of string or a mylar strip to retain the snares.

■ **Parallel and floating mechanisms** – take full advantage of the whole head-width and keep the snares at tension and independent of the shell, whether engaged with the head or not. They have sophisticated internal parallel mechanisms with several nylon and steel moving parts. The Premier one shown here has worked solidly for half a century but has precision British engineering on its side. A potential snag is the dependence on brand-specific snare wires. I carried spares for years but never needed them, though they occasionally popped out of their socket.

Alternative snare wires

You can easily customise the sound of your snare by experimenting with different wire materials and configurations.

■ Rhythm Tech offer the 'active snare', which offers a different response. Attached exactly as a conventional snare wire, the enclosing pod isolates the wires from the head and presents an interesting alternative sound – subjectively you hear the drum and the snare separately, which is unusual and may have an application for a particular tune.

■ Puresound offer steel coils and 'anti-choke' end plates.

■ Very wide 30-strand snares are also worth a try – but be aware of the limitations of your drum's snare bed and rim cavities!

In the final test, choose a snare with your ears and in context with both the rest of your kit and the music you intend to play.

Inevitably you may end up owning several snares and choosing your weapon to match the music. Just as guitarists pick a Fender for country and a Gibson for jazz, you may choose a deep snare for a power ballad and a piccolo for a fast rocker.

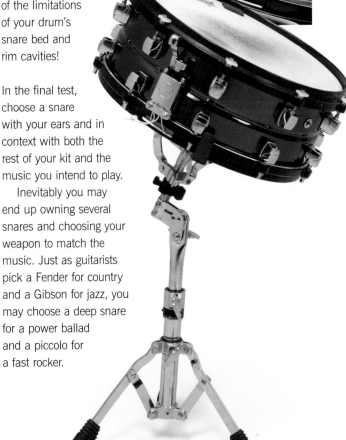

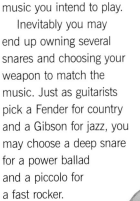

Choosing a bass drum

Choose the best drum for the job. Generally larger, deeper or taller drums deliver a lower fundamental frequency, so in the context of a kit a smaller bass drum is ideal for complex jazz accents in the style of Max Roach and Elvin Jones, and larger drums are more suited to the simple throb of rock anthems such as *We Will Rock You* – though with the right tension and suitable damping a large drum could cope well with the staccato thunder of a double-pedal fill.

Specific materials

Perceived wisdom has birch at the bright end of the spectrum and maple for rich lows – probably the reason Steve Gadd has a maple bass drum with his otherwise birch kit.

Recording and PA work

During my long spell working in a recording studio it became clear that though drums can sound very different acoustically, once we engage with the issue of recording or amplifying a drum and finding it a place in the overall mix the size of the drum becomes less critical – often smaller bass drums record better, the reason why many session drummers have favoured smaller, often Gretsch, jazz kits in the studio. The same criterion can apply when faced with close miking for live PA work.

Size matters

The rock norm has long been 20–22in, whereas Jazzers will go down to 18in and less. With the current trend for complex double-pedal fills it makes sense to think less overtones and more clarity, so smaller but possibly deeper drums make sense.

A ported
front head.

Ported heads

Many front or resonant heads are ported for microphone access and also a faster response. The large front cavity avoids air compression as the batter head moves.

Check inside

A skilled drum retailer can have a head off in less than a minute – so ask! Check for clean workmanship, avoid sloppy glue spills and overlapping joints. Are all the lugs secure? And while you're at it, soak up the lovely aroma of fresh timber!

Bearing edges

Check and avoid splinters and frayed ply. Pearl tend to a sharp 45° bearing edge for impact and calm the high frequencies with cleverly designed EQ ringed heads. Other manufacturers roll the edge for more head contact and less highs. Experiment until you find something that works for you.

Hardware

Look for substantial claw hooks with some rubberised protection for the wooden hoops.

Substantial and adjustable braced legs keep the drum upright and may also help avoid any forward creep.

I'd suggest avoiding direct tom mountings if you can, as these and the weight of the toms themselves can considerably inhibit the resonance of the shell – let the drum sing! These days there are plenty of free-standing tom stands available.

Bass drum
hoop protector.

A rim protector can be retro-fitted, but do this before mounting a pedal, as once damaged a hoop finish repair can be difficult to match.

Choosing your toms

I remember Paul McCartney saying that he chose the drummer for Wings on the basis that he went straight for the toms. Certainly, toms add the character to a kit, 'stadium' big or 'jazz' polite?

How many?

I think of toms as 'the drama department' of the kit, whether it's Gene Krupa at the beginning of the modern kit era, calling up the jungle toms of *Swing Swing Swing* or Steve Gadd playing a four-tom fill at the climax of an Eric Clapton gig. The bigger the venue and the wilder the crowd, the more the drama department comes into play. For stadium rock 12 toms is just fine, for a jam at the local bar, two might be all you need. Generally the essential groove is laid down by the bass, snare and hi-hat, and that's true for every gig – toms you can add to the recipe according to taste.

Size matters

I like to think of tom sizes in ratios. If you only have two then it's relatively easy – they can sit approximately an octave apart and fulfil different roles, the small tom for minor fills and the large tom for dramatic endings. If you have four or six it gets harder. Dr Gadd goes for 12in x 8in, 13in x 9in, 14in x 12in and 16in x 14in. This results in a natural musical progression high to low with the heads at similar tensions – very workable.

Other drummers prefer 'power toms', which are generally deeper but sometimes also with smaller diameters. These are naturally slower to respond, as the resonant head is further from the batter, but they have their compensations. Think power ballads, and the slower response is totally in keeping with the mood. For modern jazz down the local pub a faster, brighter response is going to sit more comfortably with the band. So that's two kits, then!

Resonant heads

The present norm is to err towards a coated batter and a thin clear resonance, but this may not be the easiest attuning arrangement – try experimenting with matched heads, especially if you like the sound of a 'consonant' drum (in tune with itself).

Concert toms

The 1970s trend for single-headed 'concert toms' was largely driven by under-head miking techniques and sits well in a classic '70s mix – usually needing some hefty reverb to make up for their inherent short decay. If it's a stadium and somebody else is carrying your drums, then go for both!

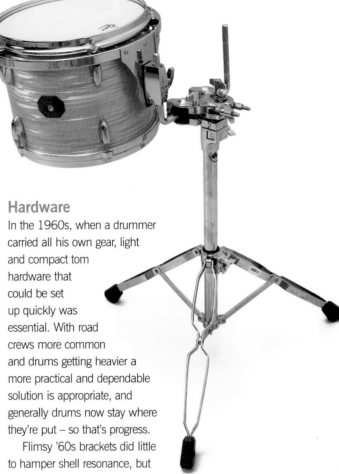

Hardware

In the 1960s, when a drummer carried all his own gear, light and compact tom hardware that could be set up quickly was essential. With road crews more common and drums getting heavier a more practical and dependable solution is appropriate, and generally drums now stay where they're put – so that's progress.

Flimsy '60s brackets did little to hamper shell resonance, but the heavy artillery and extra mounted tom did much to squash the '70s bass drum and still does. However, Steve Gadd puts so much extra damping in his bass drum to get his well-defined sound that it hardly matters.

Gary Gauger was the first to suggest toms might sound better without all this metalwork, and whilst you're at it let's free up the bass drum – Gary's RIMS are now ubiquitous; see page 90 for more on these.

Tom racks were very fashionable for a time and gave extreme flexibility for the whole kit. They're ideal for five or six toms, but the extra scaffolding really precludes most gigging drummers.

Getting started

Having agonised over birch versus maple, and rationalised the scale of things from nine toms to three, you are now burning to get playing!

Take your time, especially if you have to do the assembly from scratch. Proper seating and tensioning of the heads is crucial to the sound of your kit, and if you don't like the component sounds, you will loathe the kit.

Take special care over threads and lubricants – it is very easy to strip a thread, especially on economy kits, and a crossed thread may delay things for days.

Enjoy the assembly and tensioning, as this is the best way to understand your kit and discover your own unique sound.

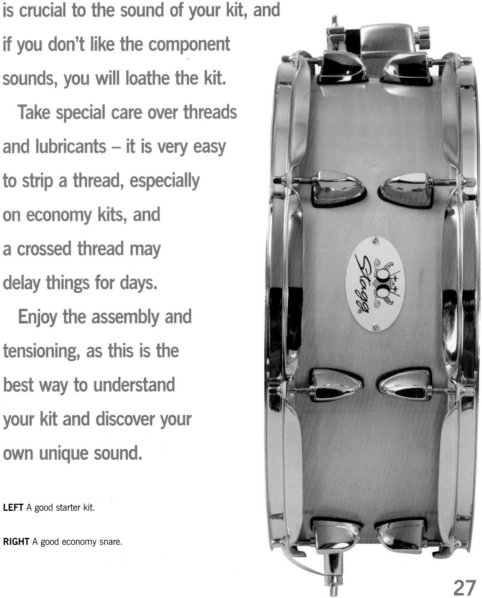

LEFT A good starter kit.

RIGHT A good economy snare.

Assembly

Ideally you should buy your kit from a reputable retailer, who'll assemble and check the kit at his premises and offer advice on ancillaries such as sticks and gig bags. The case for the music shop is still very strong.

However, if you buy on the Internet many new drum kits currently arrive as a 'flat-pack' – not strictly very flat, but nevertheless compacted. This means that the would-be drummer has first to be a drum technician and install the heads and fittings that turn a set of components into a viable instrument.

On the negative side this slows you down, but the *positive* side is that it's a great intro to understanding the mechanics of the kit.

■ To save space the drums are often packed concentrically – the toms within the bass drum shell.

■ In this instance a second box contains the fully assembled snare and individually packed stands.

■ This means that you probably only have to install one head on each drum and you have a model to work from in viewing both the other head and the fully assembled snare.

■ Take the time to check that all of the lugs are tight – this often requires a No 2 Pozidrive screwdriver. These bolts often work loose due to post-manufacture shrinkage.

■ You can make attuning the drums easier by rubbing a smear of candle wax over the bearing edges of all the shells before assembly – this makes for smooth and even friction-free tensioning.

■ Applying a little Vaseline or Lubrikit in the bolt threads will both save the threads and make for smoother attuning. The syringe makes this easier.

■ The crucial thing is to take your time and be methodical.

Above all avoid putting uneven tension on any of the hoops or heads, as the resulting distortion can be very difficult to remedy.

■ The process of assembly is relatively straightforward – head over shell, and then hoop over head. Take care to align the bolt-holes with the lugs.

■ Add the 'tuning' bolts all round the hoop (not forgetting the washers), but don't actually tension these yet – just engage a few threads.

■ Then tension the bolts just flush to the hoop. It's safer to do this by hand, as you can feel when tension is starting to engage – *and stop*.

■ Once the head is evenly engaged with the hoop, you can tension the head a quarter-turn all round in the bolt order shown above.

■ Another half-turn should take any loose ripples from the head.

■ A gentle centre squeeze should help seat the head evenly. As regards tensioning, see page 30 for fine-tuning procedures.

Fixtures and fittings

All drum manufacturers have their own ideas regarding the detail of stands and fittings, but generally they're all fairly obvious in their assembly. For more detail on these issues please refer to the brand-specific case studies later in this book.

One issue that may catch out unwary beginners, however, is the 'memory lock'. These useful aides to consistent assembly must be de-tensioned with a drum key *prior to initial assembly*. Once a suitable setting has been established they can usefully be left in situ, 'memorising' your favourite heights and angles.

✒ Pro Tip

I like to tension the head very high and then bring it down to a working tension.

Steve Gadd

Sound and tensioning 1: the toms

As a kit drummer I find it's more helpful on the whole to refer to tensioning and attuning a kit rather than 'tuning' – tuning suggests a defined pitch such as concert A = 440Hz, as with a classical timpani drum. I did do that at college, but as we all know, the modern drum kit is more likely attuned for timbre and tone colour rather than absolute pitch.

Also, a well-attuned sound from a kit is really about context, and it's hard to abstract that. As a gigging teenage drummer I realised that on any one night a specific tom could sound great and the next it would only sound OK; the same could be said for most of the kit. This used to puzzle me. With hindsight I realise that these drums were being heard subject to a lot of changes:

- Temperature – hot stages and cold vans.
- Humidity – damp humid clubs, freezing exteriors.
- Acoustics – one club is a dungeon made of stone, the next a gym hall made of wood.
- Different venues would suggest different sets of songs from the band, and one drum sound didn't necessarily fit all tunes.

Pro Tip

Tuning isn't about a note, it's about getting a drum to sound good in a certain room; it's trial and error, but there are certain fundamentals – an ambassador coated on top and a clear resonant gives the drum a little more resonance.

Steve Gadd

Admittedly we can't often change these factors, but realising they exist we can have a strategy geared up to quickly get the best from any kit in any situation. Most of what follows refers to double-headed drums, but single-headers follow much the same principles.

When I began playing in the 1950s, drums had calf 'skins', whereas since the '60s they've usually had plastic heads. In drum-speak the 'batter' is generally the one that's struck and the 'resonant' is often referred to as the bottom head.

We're starting with the toms because, without snares and complex damping issues to divert us, these are the simplest drums on which to experiment with sound. As I said earlier, toms are the drama department of the kit – *'Look out, it's a tom fill! Here comes the chorus!'* – and err towards the most dramatic sound I can get.

First of all we need to get the best possible 'starting sound' from each specific tom:

- Evaluate the drum and choose a suitable head – generally a small drum has a higher fundamental frequency and limited resonance. This is likely to respond well, fitted with a light, un-damped, single-ply head.
- Conversely, a large drum with masses of resonance may need some taming to make it manageable – so a double-ply head with some built-in damping could be appropriate.
- However, these are just two extremes and there are many more options these days. Be prepared to experiment over the lifetime of the drum, and be aware that batter heads and resonant heads need not be identical and that every drum has its own character, as long as it blends with the kit.
- Buy the best heads you can possibly afford – good heads can make inexpensive drums come to life. (See page 82 onwards for much more on heads.)

Replacing the tom heads

Old pitted and stretched heads are often difficult to attune, so start with decent new heads. I recommend starting with the lowest tom and working up to the highest – avoiding the risk of not being able to get the lowest tom sounding 'low' enough! – you can always raise the tension of the higher tom.

1 Remove the old batter head, carefully de-tensioning the hoop evenly and in rotation as shown; this not only preserves the hoop integrity but also puts even strain on the lug threads.

2 Note this is a six-lug drum, but the same de-tensioning principle would apply to an eight- or ten-lug.

3 Once the bolts are free of the head I use an Evans 'Bit Key' in my electric screwdriver to speed up their removal – this is a drum key with a normal screwdriver-chuck adaptor.

4 Place the hoop with its bolts intact on a drum stool – this saves losing any washers etc.

5 Check the bearing edge for anything uneven – rough glue pushed out from the ply is common on many new drums and can cause an uneven surface and tensioning problems.

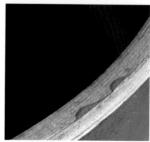

✎ Pro Tip

I find it useful to make a note of the existing tension on any head as a reference point – especially if you like the sound (the British 'Drum Tuna' with its digital readout is invaluable for this) – giving me an accurate guide to the *actual* head tension at every lug. The Tuna is 'zeroed' on a hard flat surface (my straight edge) and then provides a reference figure for the plasticity of any given head, at any point – less plasticity = higher tension.

Frank Marvel

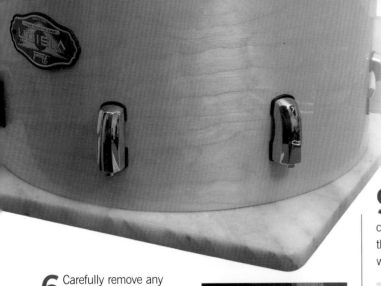

6 Carefully remove any excess dry glue without splintering the wood; a very mild abrasive paper should take off the glue and leave the bearing edge intact – I'm using 3M281Q wet or dry. **NB** You should only do this if you have a level surface as a reference, such as a tile or the marble slab in these pictures. You must avoid creating any low spots on the edge, as this would make tensioning a nightmare.

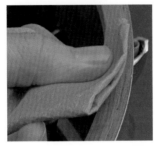

7 When using a flat plate, a light bulb placed inside the drum can help reveal any imperfections.

8 If the bearing edge is very uneven you should consult a drum tech via your local music shop, since you need specialist tools to guarantee a good even cut.

⚡ Pro Tip

If you're in any doubt about tools and methods, take the drum to a qualified drum tech. A drum with a badly damaged bearing edge is probably an ex-drum.

Frank Marvel

---

9 Lubricate the bearing edge with a little candle wax. This will help the head move smoothly when tensioning.

10 Apply the new head – aligning the head badge with the shell badge can provide a useful reference point.

11 Check that the head is seating properly and moving freely on the bearing edge.

12 Discard the old head, check the hoop is clean, then reapply the hoop, aligning it with the lugs.

13 Fit the bolts, not forgetting a washer for each (nylon is smoother and may help keep the bolt from detuning, but they'll need replacing more often).

14 Take up the slack on the bolts and leave them just touching the hoop. Check again for even head seating.

15 Apply a full turn to each bolt using the same cross-diagonal pattern as before.

16 Seat the head using some gentle pressure, as shown. The bigger the drum, the more pressure may be required.

17 Try another quarter-turn all round and then listen to the head with the resonant head muted by a fluffy towel (the *Spinal Tap* variety).

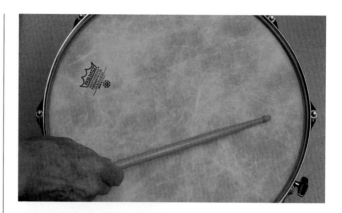

18 Playing 'off' the head, 1–2in in from the edge, should reveal a similar pitch at each bolt. If you have a drum Tuna or similar you can apply a little science to achieve exactly the same tension at each bolt.

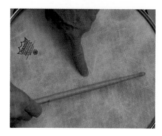

19 A finger applied gently at the centre of the drum will reduce the fundamental resonance and enable you to better hear the individual 'pitches' at the lugs.

20 Tension the drum another half-turn and check the pitches again all around the rim (one-and-a-half turns total, leaving the head quite low-pitched). Repeat the procedure for the resonant head.

Once both heads are at the same tension listen to the overall sound with the drum in its playing mount or on its stand as it will be heard on stage – mounting toms on or even near a bass drum will excite resonance in the bass drum and alter the overall perception of the tom sound; an adjacent tom will also excite sympathetic vibration, so attuning a drum in isolation is a bit academic. Sympathetic vibration is part of what makes a kit exciting, so this not a negative.

■ **Listen**

If things go to plan the drum should sound open and resonant with one consonant overtone dominant. You then decide if it's too low or too high in relation to your other toms and the music you're going to play, and re-tension both heads accordingly.

Non-consistent tension

Other options include tuning the resonant head lower than the batter – which can give a longer sustain and often a 'pitch' glissandi effect ('down' then 'up'), which can sound good in certain contexts – or tuning the resonant higher than the batter, which often gives a faster and shorter response. These choices are matters of taste and what makes your sound your own, so experiment and dare to be different.

Find the fundamental resonance

When experimenting with tension you often discover the 'sweet spot' for a particular drum – when the whole drum shell and heads respond at their fundamental resonance – this can be either brilliant and usable or a distracting nuisance, depending on the blend with the other drums; but either way, when you find this resonant point make a note of the tension required and use it as a reference point for future tunings. Pro Torq drum keys can be used here; these are much cheaper but naturally cruder than the Drum Tuna; they work by detecting the torque experienced at the lug bolt and giving you a replicable 'number' for that torque.

Neary Drum Torque

Another more sophisticated device is the Regal Tip Neary Drum Torque, which gives you a more accurate measurement of the torque of each tension bolt. Be aware, however, that poorly lubricated or corroded

bolts may register varying torque – consequently Regal Tip recommend lubricating and checking the smooth-running of every bolt before attempting to measure the torque. I personally prefer to measure or listen to the *actual* head tension. The Neary has interchangeable bits to cope with standard square tension bolts and bass drum timpani tuners.

Matching toms

Once you have a sound you like on the lowest tom work up to the next tom and try a similar tension, but on a smaller shell – in a well-matched set of toms this will give you a good starting point. Many drummers attune a two-tom set-up to have a distinct wide gap between their fundamental notes; this makes sense and makes for a more dramatic contrast in two-tom fills. Naturally this gets harder to achieve with three- and four-tom set-ups, as the gaps tend to close between the fundamental tones. However, well-designed modern kits take this factor into account and good distinct 'notes' should be achievable with good heads and a little patient experimentation.

You may need to apply a little damping to the batter head in certain situations, especially recording – see pages 41 (damping) and 96 (recording).

You'll have arrived as a musician drummer when you know your drums well enough to get good results consistently in varying stage and studio acoustics. This will take time and a lot of experimentation, but it's all part of the learning process and defines your personality as heard by the band and the audience. Enjoy it.

Sound and tensioning 2: the snare

Everything that applied to the toms in the previous chapter applies to the snare. This is because when Gene Krupa asked Slingerland for a set of tunable toms in 1934, in practical terms they were really creating a set of snare drums *without snares*.

Both drums also have their roots on the battlefield; before the days of radio communication the snared gut was the key signalling device, its coded messages cutting through the roar of battle. The toms were tenor drums stirring the foot soldiers to acts of dramatic bravery.

Now the snare cuts through the roar of rock and the blare of jazz, laying down a regimental groove on the backbeat.

'Cutting through' generally requires a piercing transient, provided on the battlefield by stretched gut against the resonant head, these days replaced by a set of tensioned wires. A higher tension at the heads also helps place most of the snare drum's sonic energy in the 1–10khz band where our ears are at their most sensitive.

Typically a snare drum head might be at twice the tension of the toms.

Choose a head

■ Traditionally the snare head was calfskin and had a natural texture that both made for effective wire-brush work and was naturally 'damped'.

■ With the introduction of mylar (an adapted photographic negative material) the head was at first incredibly glass-smooth. Then, after a brief period when drummers were invited to DIY-spray a rough texture on their snares, the Remo-coated head appeared. Again the coating not only makes brushwork possible but also attenuates the higher partials, putting the drum sound into a more useful range.

■ Double-ply heads and Fiberskyn heads offer more damping and tend to mellow the snare. Useful for many applications.

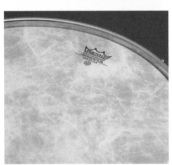

■ 'Reverse Dot' snare heads may help focus the drum's fundamental frequency for a thicker driving backbeat.

■ For the resonant head most drummers now err towards a clear, very thin head for maximum responsiveness and sensitivity.

Tensioning

Initially follow the lug tension guidelines as outlined for the toms.

However, using a Drum Tuna or similar gauge gives us a graphic guide to the higher tension of a typical snare batter, .002in reflecting very little give in the head. When using a Tuna or torque gauge to aid tensioning the resonant head be aware that the snare bed commonly found on the shell will result in more elasticity at the lugs adjacent to the snare, giving higher readings – the resonant here is generally reading .08in, but .09in at the snare bed area, reflecting the lower tension.

Similar tensions on the snare batter and resonant will again result in a consonant synergy and often a louder drum. Experiment in order to find the resonant frequency of your snare – the point at which the drum 'comes alive' and the heads and shell work as a complementary system. Once this is found, keep a note of the tensions as this is a useful reference point, even if you occasionally want the drum to be less explosive and you tension away from the fundamental resonance. Be aware that different heads will affect this resonance point, so be consistent when buying new heads.

Dave Mattacks, one of Britain's finest session drummers (though now based in the USA), has a unique and interesting approach to the snare:

'I sometimes do an unusual thing to the batter head. Assuming the rod nearest you is the six o'clock position and the one furthest away (closest to the rack tom) the 12 o'clock, I tension the "12" a couple of turns tighter, the "11" and "1" positions one-and-a-half turns tighter, and the "10" and "2" one turn tighter. The "3" and "9" remain as is; then the "4" and "8" are one-and-a-half turns looser, the "5" and "7" one turn looser, and finally the "6" two turns looser. This is all relative, whether you've a ten- or eight-lug drum, and has several effects. Firstly it still gives a good playing response centre-head; secondly it dampens the drum slightly, and finally and most importantly – because the head tension is at its lowest near to you – it gives depth to rimshots.'

Most drummers will use some extra damping on the snare batter, especially in recording situations. (See page 41 for more on this, and also see the Steve Gadd case study on page 164.)

Sound and tensioning 3: the bass drum

In the development of the drum kit, approaches to bass drum sounds have been heavily influenced by the dynamic limitations of recording and broadcasting.

Initially the pioneers of cylinder and 78rpm recordings deemed such bass drums unrecordable; the range of frequencies (20Hz–20Khz), the transient impact and the sheer volume swamped early audio horns and microphones and prompted an outright ban from the fledgling studio.

If you listen to the 1918 recordings of the Original Dixieland Jazz band, the bass drum is conspicuous by its absence. For *Tiger Rag*, drummer Tony Sbarbaro has to rely on woodblocks, cowbells and a polite china cymbal to drive what was probably a raucous live band. This recording limitation may have even prolonged the life and diversity of the contraption kit, Sbarbaro later adding a mounted kazoo to his armoury. The situation had improved little by 1927, when Gene Krupa finally persuaded Okeh records that a bass drum and a tom *could* be recorded, with some judicious muffling provided by a well-placed rug. This marks a change in what was from then on perceived as a 'bass drum'.

A little perspective

The drum kit developed alongside jazz, and jazz was amongst the first popular music to be recorded. The first 'Jass' bass drums were up to 30in tall, narrow-shelled whoppers borrowed from the New Orleans marching bands. These calf-skinned giants packed the sort of thump that could inspire any army to battle. This fine specimen belongs to Her Majesty's Horse Guards.

Practicalities: a 'modern' approach batter head

1 Do all the usual checks whilst the batter head is off: tighten all the lug screws and check the bearing edge. (See routine maintenance in the case studies for more on these issues.)

2 Fit the new head and bring to the lowest possible tension commensurate with losing the wrinkles. Tighten diagonally in sequence as with the toms and snare.

3 The new heads may need considerable stretching – some drummers actually stand on the head for this, though I find a good, even centre-push usually suffices.

4 After stretching, slowly remove the wrinkles again with a half-turn all round – the apparent wrinkles in this head are actually on the internal damping ring.

Right through the analogue recording era, cutting engineers would fret over bass drums literally throwing the gramophone needle out of the groove. Consequently, on the studio floor bass drums would be swathed in blankets, front heads removed and bricks and stage weights braced against batter heads. In the studio control room the engineer's armoury of dynamic compression and broad-band equalisation turned a bass drum into a 'click' with a dynamic range of 1dB. This click worked well on mono AM Radio, where bass frequencies were limited, and the click became the accepted sound of the 'kick' drum – not just in recording but eventually *on the stage*.

Bass drums got smaller, and Ringo Starr and every other drummer of the '50s and '60s had to put up with such emasculated bass drums. John Bonham's producer Jimmy Page, working with Hendrix engineer Eddie Kramer, eventually challenged the grip with *Whole Lotta Love*, on the *Led Zeppelin II* album, and sent a million styli jumping from the groove – a rebel call.

However, by now most people – including many musicians – thought a bass drum naturally made a subdued click, and '80s 'electronica' sampled that click for the future.

Thankfully the arrival of digital recording and growth of stereo FM radio made it feasible to record a broader band of frequencies. The digital revolution even offered a dynamic range extended to 90dB. There's definitely something approaching a bass drum on Dire Straits' CD-defining *Brothers In Arms*.

Drummer Steve Gadd is one amongst many who have seized the potential of the modern recording studio and wide-band PA to finally reinstate the bass drum as a true bass voice centre-stage – two heads back almost intact.

5 Bear in mind that where the bass drum is internally damped a mechanical tuning device such as the Drum Tuna may be thrown by the natural change in resistance.

6 Assuming you're happy with the resonant head the next step is to listen to the new head at this lowest tension.

Experiment with types of beater

■ Try a variety of beaters and experiment with the striking area, as these factors combined with the damping applied can change the sound of the drum dramatically. (See the next chapter for more on bass-drum damping.)

■ A wooden beater will bring out more of a transient than a lambswool or felt beater, and a modern hard plastic beater will work well in double-pedal situations where clarity is needed for very fast staccato beats. Striking in the middle of the head excites more lows and less of the higher harmonics. As you move towards the hoop you lose some power, but can gain some clarity.

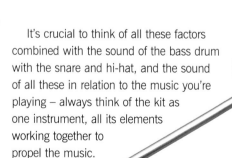

It's crucial to think of all these factors combined with the sound of the bass drum with the snare and hi-hat, and the sound of all these in relation to the music you're playing – always think of the kit as one instrument, all its elements working together to propel the music.

ABOVE A lifetime's collection of bass drum beaters.

Resonant head

Generally the modern resonant head is ported, and the positioning and size of the port are also very critical.

■ A large port in the centre will give the effect of having virtually no resonant head.

■ A smaller port set towards the hoop will allow the head to resonate but also allow microphone access.

■ A further advantage of porting is that it reduces the compression caused when the beater strikes the batter head. (See page 45 for more on porting.)

■ Tensioning the resonant head higher than the batter will generally extend the sustain of the 'note', and having it looser will give it more staccato punch.

■ It's again worth finding the resonant frequency of the bass drum – though this may eventually need taming for discrimination between beats – since it will be a great starting point for your sound. Try similar low tensions on both heads and then experiment a little until the drum hopefully comes to life. You may need to try several types of head combination before you're happy (see page 82). Once you've found the resonant frequency, see the next chapter for any necessary damping.

Controlling harmonics and resonance

Getting the best from any drum set is often about getting a good core sound and then controlling and balancing excess resonance and harmonics. We want our drums to sound dramatic and dynamic, *not* out of control. We also want the kit to blend into one harmonious unit, with no one drum standing out and spoiling the overall effect. This can often mean a little subtle head-damping.

Mechanicals

From the 1920s on various mechanical dampers became available – usually lambswool pads attached to metal discs. These looked awful and messed up your hoops. They were, however, quite effective.

Eventually these were offered as internal dampers, and their shape changed to felt pads rather than discs.

Unfortunately, though adjustable these pads are a bit crude in their effect, and not very flexible – in practice they are sort of 'on' or 'off'. They also push up against the head, distorting the even tension at one point in the hoop.

Tone rings

If you're trying to bring out the fundamental note of the drum, 'tone rings' – simple hoops of mylar – gently mute the rim harmonics and subjectively let us hear more of that fundamental. These are used very effectively by Steve Gadd on his snare – that's what gives the tight 'military' sound on the intro to *50 Ways to Lose Your Lover*. Steve always remembers to deftly remove his ring before switching to brushes – they otherwise catch on the wire! Tone rings are available as 'sets' from many manufacturers. They're like double-ply heads, but removable for tunes that need a more 'open' sound.

■ DIY tone rings

You can make your own 'custom' tone rings from old heads. Simply cut off the hoop and the centre and modify to your preferred amount of damping. Always cut away from those paradiddle digits! The pinstripe on this old 'pinstripe Remo' makes a useful cutting guide – you could simply substitute a plate or cymbal of an appropriate diameter. Avoid using old heads with too many dents and creases as these can rattle annoyingly against the new head. You can leave a *little* shoulder on the new ring to keep it still on the drum, but leave too much and it will sit proud. The double-ply pinstripe makes for more substantial damping; a single ply makes for another option.

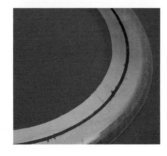

Externally-mounted adjustable damping

'EMAD' is a product from Evans, the renowned head manufacturer. These simple self-adhesive Velcro strips are tidier than gaffer tape and can offer a range of damping effects depending on where they're attached.

1 It's important to clean the surface before attaching, as grease will cause the pads to fall off at the wrong moment. An alcohol wipe is provided in the EMAD pack.

2 Secure the EMAD on the rim by removing the wax paper from the adhesive.

3 Locate the other end of the pad on the head as required – experiment before securing hard on the head.

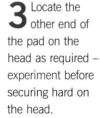

4 The EMAD will attach to itself when not required.

EMAD works well for subtle control of edge harmonics – not quite as severe as a tone ring. They're probably most useful in the studio.

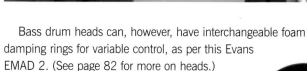

Heads with built-in damping

These can be a great idea if you have one set sound in mind for a specific gig – but you need to be sure they're versatile enough for the range of music you're playing; be aware that they're intrinsically 'fixed' – you can add *more* damping, but you can't make the heads less damped. Oil-filled double-ply heads are one example; this is an Evans TT 16 GT (the rainbow effect being the trapped oil).

This EC1 'Reverse Dot' has a damping foil dot under the centre and a high harmonic damping ring under the outer edge.

Bass drum heads can, however, have interchangeable foam damping rings for variable control, as per this Evans EMAD 2. (See page 82 for more on heads.)

Moongel

A popular approach to damping, Moongel from RTOM is a self-adhesive gel that sticks to the surface of drums, cymbals and most other percussion instruments. Moving the damper pad around the surface controls unwanted resonance, and customises your drum sound to suit the specific acoustic of the room. This example is Steve Gadd's snare-drum arrangement for an Eric Clapton tour.

The soft non-toxic gel is packaged in a durable plastic container. It's particularly popular in recording situations for subtle modifications to individual drums. Moongel is washable and will retain its stickiness for years.

The gel can be cut to size – small for situations that call for a minimum amount of damping. For *maximum* resonance control you could try one damper pad at twelve o'clock or six o'clock, and a second damper pad at 3 o'clock or 9 o'clock.

Damping the bass drum

One modern approach is the Evans EQ Pad – drummers used a blanket for the same results until very recently, but this approach is more flexible and less drastic! The EQ Pad lifts slightly when the head is struck and then returns to full damping – simple and ingenious. It has two levels of damping as supplied and is simply attached by Velcro. If you need more damping there's an extra RGS 'gate' (a pillow) which attaches to the EQ Pad.

LEFT Steve Gadd's solution.

■ Retro bass drum sounds

For 1960s and '70s heavily damped bass drum sounds you should experiment with double-ply batter heads. Removing or heavily porting the resonant head will also be necessary. A blanket folded against the head inside the shell and suitably restrained with a weight will give that period 'click'. Try to avoid the 'stage weight' extreme approach, as these are heavy enough to distort the shell. Here I'm recycling some old NiCad batteries – heavy, but not *too* heavy.

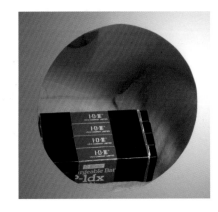

An AKG D112 dynamic microphone halfway into the shell coupled with 10:1 limiting and 1kHz and 4Khz peaks in the PA EQ should set your '70s flares flapping!

Steve Gadd uses a removal contractor's blanket strapped into shape, extremely heavy and stable.

Bass drum porting

Ideally your bass drum has two complete heads, a batter and a resonant. This offers the most volume and resonance from the drum. In the last few decades, however, removing the resonant head for the convenience of placing a microphone for recording and PA work has led to a common misconception that the front head is merely a nuisance.

■ A large hole in the centre will minimise the effect of the resonant head but is less drastic than removing the head and hoop completely.

■ A smaller hole will retain much of the effect of the resonant head, especially if it's placed off-centre, leaving the fundamental resonance more intact.

■ Four o'clock position (as below) and eight o'clock position leave less microphone cable hanging against the drum head, and also leave plenty of space above for band logos etc.

ABOVE One radical solution is the 'Drumport' which replaces the front head with an acoustic 'lens', giving a very modern, focused sound.

A good compromise is a simple hole in the batter head. This not only provides access for a microphone aimed at getting the optimum 'click' transient from the batter, but also reduces the compression effect when the batter head moves inwards to accommodate the impact of the bass drum beater.

The size and position of this hole will affect the sound:

Making your own port

I strongly recommend that you line any resonant head hole to avoid tearing by microphone cables and overenthusiastic road crew. Proprietary 'Bass Drum O's' are simple self-adhesive metal and plastic rims that do the job nicely. There are several brands on the market.

They're available in a range of sizes and colours: red chrome, green chrome, blue chrome and purple chrome. The 2in sizes are also available in silver chrome, black, white and brass. The 2in ports are unsuitable for microphone use and simply act as compression ports. In addition 4in, 5in and 6in sizes are available, plus 6in x 4in ovals.

Here I'm installing a 5in – big enough to allow microphone access, but not big enough to spoil the head resonance:

1 First remove the head and place this rim, edge-up, on a clean level surface.

2 Select the area on the drumhead where the 'O' is to be installed. Allow a margin of at least 2in from the outside edge of the 'O' to the rim.

3 You may want to mark up the area with a pencil or pen.

4 Clean the area of the head using an alcohol wipe. 'O' rings supply one, but the medical swabs available from a drugstore or chemist will also do the job.

5 Wipe the surface dry with a soft cotton cloth. This will help adhesion and avoid any potential 'rattle'.

6 Remove the protective waxed paper ring on the 'female' piece. Avoiding touching the exposed adhesive, place the female piece – gasket side down – on the area of the head you've selected. Press firmly, making sure that the glue adheres completely and evenly. Check for air gaps on the clear heads by examining the opposite side of the head.

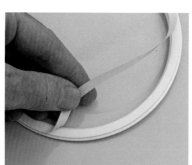

Cut the hole

7 Lift the head from the table. Using a sharp knife (a Stanley or an X-Acto will do the job), make the incision from the front of the head up against and parallel to the inside edge of the 'female' ring.

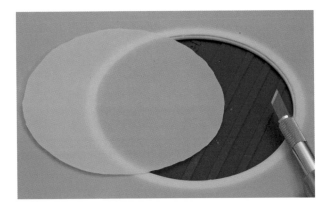

8 At an approximately 20° angle to the 'O', cut along the inside edge of the female ring. Avoid cutting into the ring itself. Complete the circle and remove the hole. Take care not to tear the head as you ease the plastic out.

Male piece

9 As before, clean the front of the drumhead where the ring will adhere, then wipe dry with a cotton rag.

10 Remove the protective waxed paper ring on the male piece. Moisten the gasket and snap lip with the alcohol wipe. This allows the outer ring to slip easily into place and adhere better.

11 Place outer ring face-down on the table. Fit one side of the female ring under the lip of the snap groove on the male ring. Make sure the female ring edge is pushed completely under the lip of the snap groove on the male ring. The two ring edges must line up.

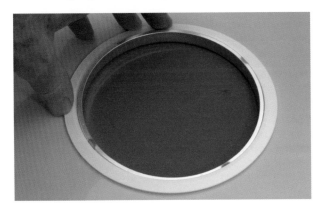

12 Using one hand, hold the female ring edge firmly under the lip of the snap groove on the male ring. Using your free hand, press around the female ring until the entire ring is locked under the snap groove lip.

13 The finished job looks neat and will protect the head from any accidental snagging.

✎ Tech Tip

If you're doing a lot of port cutting a pro tool is available from some retailers which will cut an exact 2–10in hole. This has an adjustable centre pivot and a built-in revolving cutter.

Frank Marvel

Installing a bass drum KickPort

Extending the port cavity into the shell using a KickPort may have some beneficial effects, especially on smaller bass drums. Based on the concept of the Helmholtz resonator, this may help attune the shell and heads and enhance the fundamental frequency of the complex system that constitutes any drum.

ABOVE Prior to installation.

The African *djembe* drum has exploited this Helmholtz effect for hundreds of years, and you may have noticed how a *djembe* sound changes dramatically when sat flat on the ground as opposed to raised.

As in a loudspeaker baffle, the port extension helps reduce phase cancellation effects at the head surface. However, the arithmetic of this can be extremely complex, as the size of the head, the size of the shell, the head tensions and types and the positioning of the port are all critical factors in a complex equation. Only first-hand experimentation with your drum and heads can help you decide if this works for you. Scientific tests suggest much of the benefit may be in enhancing frequencies below the 40Hz area of the audio spectrum, which is rather low for most recording and playback systems. However, any harmonics enhanced above this may be beneficial, especially in live performance.

⚡ Tech Tip

The KickPort is picky about resonant heads. If you use a damped resonant head, such as an Aquarian Regulator or Evans EMAD (with foam ring), you'll get no benefit from the KickPort until you change the head. The KickPort is essentially one piece of a system. The other piece is an undamped resonant head.

Matthew McGlynn

See Appendix for more on this.

Installation

The KickPort is a simple plastic acoustic 'lens' that's fixed to the resonant head of your bass drum via a flexible rubber gasket.

The recommended position of the KickPort is similar to any regular bass drum port – four o'clock or eight o'clock – avoiding the centre of the head.

Note also that a reinforcement ring will be needed on any head that's cut to accommodate the KickPort (a self-adhesive ring is supplied as standard). Without such a ring the port will probably rattle!

I find it easier to do this installation with the head off – you can access both sides of the head and gently coax the KickPort into position.

1 The standard KickPort requires a 5–5.5in hole in the head (see previous page for cutting instructions). This Evans Onyx comes ready ported.

2 The rubber gasket is simply pushed back on the collar.

3 The lens is then carefully threaded through the reinforced head. Take your time, as you don't want a creased or torn head.

4 The rear gasket is then flattened against the inner surface of the head – simple!

Bass drum head protectors

At the beginnings of the modern kit era, lambswool beaters on calfskin gave a warm and woolly boom, and head wear was confined to a black stain. As beaters became hard felt and then solid wood, drummers responded in the '60s with moleskin patches and rubber inner-tube cut-outs to extend head life. However, these days we're often looking at hard synthetic beaters used on relatively thin mylar, and it's time to break out aramid-fibre bulletproof vest material.

Something to consider here is the impact on sound. If you examine a North Indian *tabla* drumhead this has a central pad that contributes greatly to the drum's very focussed sound and pitch. Similarly, a bass drum head protector can work beyond an extra layer of material to being a focus point for the still important transient 'click' ingredient of the overall bass drum sound – it's this first perceived sound that places the bass drum in the groove.

Before fixing a protector, consider the material options. The Evans type above is simple cross-web aramid fibre, exaggerating the transient minimally but giving some focus.

The Danmar Power Disk Kick Pad shown below has optional very hard centre discs which exaggerate the transient to a much greater degree. It will depend on the music you're playing as to whether the additional disc is needed or not.

Evans also offer clear minimal effect versions as well as black nylon. All will have subtly different effects on the tone of your drum – I can only recommend you experiment until you find *your* sound.

■ Consider the site of the pad. Experiment with beater heights – a central hit will give maximum fundamental and easing towards the rim will bring out more of the high harmonics.

■ It's important to clean the fixing area to ensure good even adhesion – any edge lifting will add a nasty buzz to the sound. A little isopropyl alcohol from your local chemist or drugstore should do the trick. Allow this to fully evaporate before adhesion.

■ The pads then attach with their own 'high temperature aerospace' self-adhesives.

Hardware and accessories

Vintage drums are rightly coveted for their unique sound, but drum hardware is a whole different area. It's been fascinating, over the last 50 years, to watch the development of drum stands and pedals. When I started playing in 1958 my Dad's kit was full of child's construction-kit-like components that tended to fall apart. Gradually, from the 1960s to the present, all drum accessories have become more rugged, robust and skilfully engineered. This is very welcome, and actually helps us sound better – it was hell playing a kit that constantly threatened to disintegrate!

LEFT An unusual 'China' from Istanbul with a useful conventional 'bell'.

RIGHT A superbly engineered modern hi-hat stand.

Cymbal stand

Perhaps the worst sound in the world for a drummer is that of a prized Zildjian hitting the stage 'edge first'. So we should invest in a few good, stable stands.

■ The now common boom extension can be a real advantage, especially as more toms and triple-braced tripods take up the available floor space. Many manufacturers offer a 'disappearing boom' option that provides useful flexibility; the boom can retract into the main stand when not required or for transport.

■ Look for solid tilters that stay where they're put without overtightening. Check for any flaky plating, as this often leads to parts not meshing, causing slippage.

■ Look for a properly counterweighted boom that won't tip.

■ A solid height setting clamp with memory locks. These should save rigging time. The original Memriloc was another innovation of the American Rogers Drum Company.

■ At least double-braced and ideally triple-braced tripods. The best quality stands open smoothly without too much force – cheap ones are always clumsy and risk finger damage.

■ Check the weight – heavy is OK if you have a road crew, too light and they'll fall over on wobbly stage risers.

Hi-hat

The huble hi-hat can produce an infinite variety of colours and textures. Good mechanics make it easier to enjoy.

■ A solid clutch with good cymbal cushions won't fall down mid-gig.

■ A simple but effective tilt mechanism saves a 'muted' vacuum from the cymbal clash.

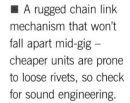

■ A solid extendable and memory-locked joint.

■ A rugged chain link mechanism that won't fall apart mid-gig – cheaper units are prone to loose rivets, so check for sound engineering.

■ Some kind of non-slip mechanism (spikes and Velcro) on the base will keep the hi-hat positioned on the drum mat – essential.

Feet

This seems elementary, but we drummers need to look after our rubber feet! These essential items are often mislaid. They not only keep drums and stands where they're put but can actually influence sound – particularly on floor toms. These Pearl 'air suspension' feet fit standard 9.5mm legs and often help isolate the resonance of a shell.

Bass drum pedal

The bass drum is the heartbeat of virtually all popular music, and as drummers we need all the help we can get to 'place' that vital anchor.

■ The evolution of the bass pedal over the last few years has been extraordinary. The first picture (left) is what I had to gig with in the early '60s (an Olympic). Ringo Starr fared quite well with this Speedking (lower right), which has internal springing concealed in the posts.

■ Modern pedals are built for speed and survival, with slightly over-engineered mechanisms – this is completely justified, as anyone who's suffered mid-gig failure will attest.

■ Adjustable lockable spring tension plus spurs and Velcro will provide the versatility and dependable positioning you need.

■ Most modern pedals are geared up to single- or double-beater arrangements. Look for rugged coupling arrangements with versatile position angles – everybody has different ideas about how the pedals should sit.

■ I like the idea of tools where you need them.

Snare stand

My first snare hung from my belt, resulting in the traditional unmatched stick grip. That marching drum tilt can still be effective.

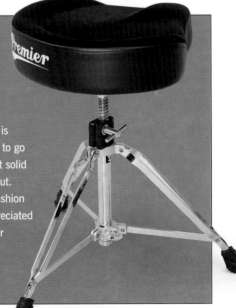

■ A solid but compact triple-braced base will ensure you can get your snare where you need it.

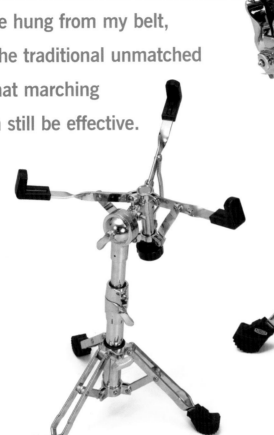

■ A well-engineered locking ball socket will give great flexibility and a rigid grip.

■ A centre tensioning basket will adjust to a wide range of snares.

A throne

■ Sit well and play well – go for comfort on any long gig.
■ The ideal throne is compact enough to go in the kit bag but solid enough to stay put.
■ A big, shaped cushion area will be appreciated after a three-hour 'ground track' session.

Pro hardware case study

If cost and weight aren't an issue and you just want the best, then the DW 9000 series is the current gold standard, though Gibraltar also offer solid alternatives, and the build of 'own brand' hardware has followed their examples.

Snare stand

This very stable triple-braced stand stays where it's put. It has a universal joint with a handy 'Techlock' that shifts on a ratchet to any useful position you might need. This acts as a cradle-tilt and complements the heavy-duty, infinitely adjustable and lockable cradle grips. It also has a very small footprint, which is useful in this era of multiple pedals.

Tom stand

This has substantial ball-joint swivel mounts for two heavy toms, and potential for an additional cymbal boom in the centre.

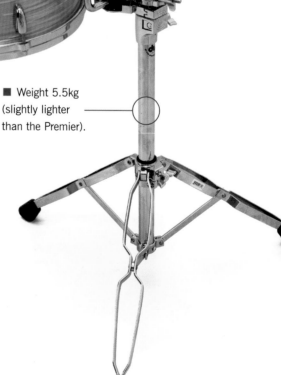

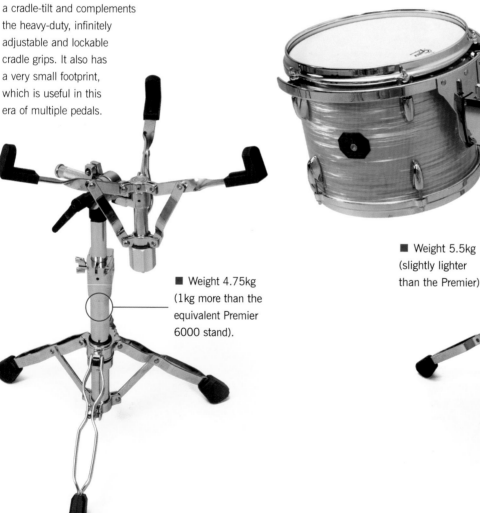

■ Weight 4.75kg (1kg more than the equivalent Premier 6000 stand).

■ Weight 5.5kg (slightly lighter than the Premier).

Hi-hat stand

Steve Gadd's favourite, this features an easy-to-use locking and infinitely variable tension adjuster, which gives a flexible choice of hi-hat response. With a solid base plate, triple chain drives and Velcro and spike position stabilisers, on any decent drum mat this hi-hat will stay where it's put.

The bottom cymbal tilt mechanism is also wing-nut lockable for consistency of set-up. The top cymbal position will also lock.

Drop clutch arrangement

This is from Gibraltar – another great hardware supplier – and can be very useful when you need a closed hi-hat sound and have both feet tied up with bass drum pedals. The clutch automatically locks the hi-hat cymbals closed when triggered on the fly mid-song.

■ Operation

1 Set the drop clutch up in the same way as any hi-hat clutch but with the lever section connected to the conventional top cymbal clamp via the 'hook' – the hi-hat will perform as normal.

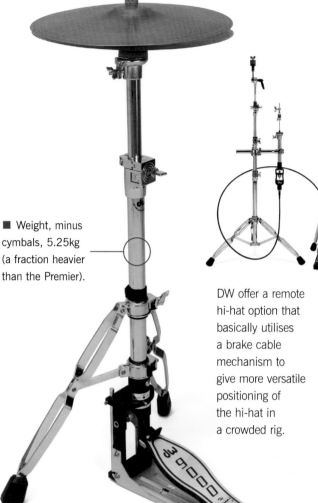

■ Weight, minus cymbals, 5.25kg (a fraction heavier than the Premier).

DW offer a remote hi-hat option that basically utilises a brake cable mechanism to give more versatile positioning of the hi-hat in a crowded rig.

2 When you need a semi-permanent 'closed' hi-hat sound, tap the black lever and the top cymbal is released. **NB** If you keep your foot on the pedal this can be achieved without a disruptive cymbal clash. The top cymbal is held in the 'down' position by the hook.

3 To re-engage the cymbal for normal use, you simply have to press down on the hi-hat pedal and it automatically re-engages with the top clutch and, hey presto, you're back to normal. Simple but effective.

Bass drum pedals

The pedal was DW's first flagship product and it maintains its industry-standard status. It has a dual chain drive with infinitely adjustable cam, dual-sided beaters and a sturdy base plate with grip spurs and Velcro grip. There is also a fully adjustable linkage to a second pedal, twin springs with infinite torque adjustment and all the necessary adjustment tools attached.

■ Weight 2.75kg each (the left-hand pedal is a fraction lighter).

A big feature of this and the hi-hat is DW's patented hinge, which has precision roller bearings for low resistance and reliability. This is accessed for lubrication with two 3/8in socket wrenches. Everything about this pedal screams rugged reliability and professional performance.

■ Tech Comment

'That hinge is very important – when you've got a heel casting and a foot board you need a hinge in between. We were the first ones to put bearings on a hinge for a foot pedal – the ball-bearing hinge. The hinge is aluminium, and we use this to take some of the weight of the pedal. The same applies to the DW hi-hat.'
John Good, senior executive vice president DW Drums

Bass drum 'pedal riser'

This useful device puts the beater strike in the right place when working with smaller bass drums, and also helps if you like the bass drum suspended off the ground. The riser is fitted to the batter hoop with a 5mm Allen wrench. The pedal fits to the wing-nut adjustable lower mount, and the beater can then be used conventionally.

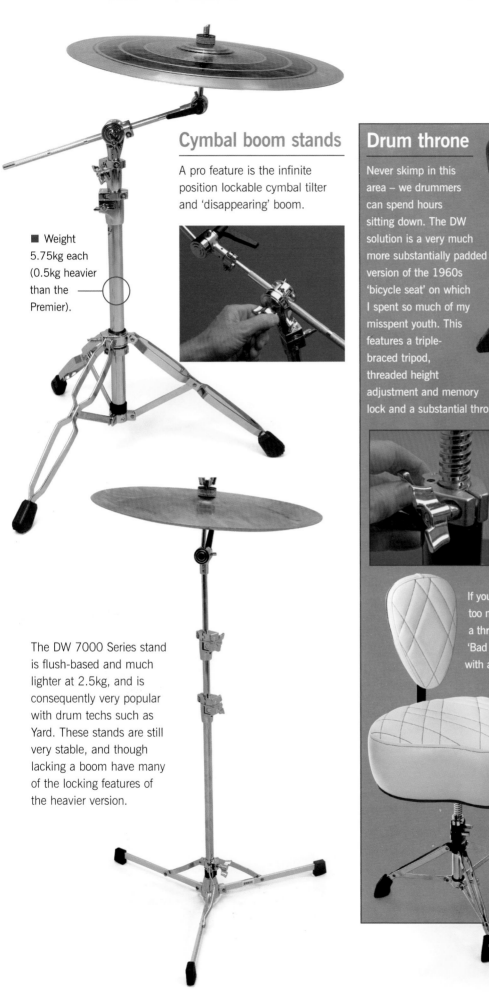

Cymbal boom stands

A pro feature is the infinite position lockable cymbal tilter and 'disappearing' boom.

■ Weight 5.75kg each (0.5kg heavier than the Premier).

The DW 7000 Series stand is flush-based and much lighter at 2.5kg, and is consequently very popular with drum techs such as Yard. These stands are still very stable, and though lacking a boom have many of the locking features of the heavier version.

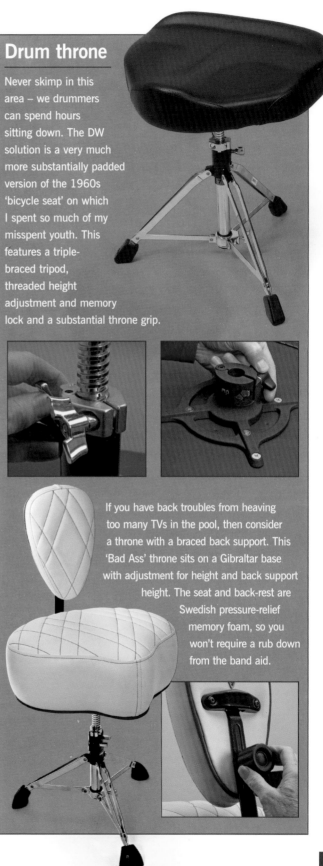

Drum throne

Never skimp in this area – we drummers can spend hours sitting down. The DW solution is a very much more substantially padded version of the 1960s 'bicycle seat' on which I spent so much of my misspent youth. This features a triple-braced tripod, threaded height adjustment and memory lock and a substantial throne grip.

If you have back troubles from heaving too many TVs in the pool, then consider a throne with a braced back support. This 'Bad Ass' throne sits on a Gibraltar base with adjustment for height and back support height. The seat and back-rest are Swedish pressure-relief memory foam, so you won't require a rub down from the band aid.

Choosing and buying cymbals

The engine room of the groove requires a good snare, a bass drum and crucially four cymbals – a pair of hi-hats, a 'ride' to lay down the beats and a crash for accents, explosive or subtle.

A good pair of hi-hats

As all drummers know, the hi-hat is an incredibly sophisticated instrument which by the nature of individual cymbal character and interaction can produce at least seven distinct sounds:

- The closed pair 'top' and 'edge', sticked.
- The open sticked 'crash' of the top cymbal.
- The loose pair – half depressed at the pedal
  – sticked 'top' and 'edge'.
- The 'chick' of the pedal-only operation.
- The rhythmically combined sound of stick and pedal.

All the above can be infinitely combined and shuffled to give a fantastic array of rhythmic colour. We all have our own taste in cymbals, and that establishes our individual sound, but a good set of hi-hats needs to respond well with all these techniques.

RIGHT Zildjian has a well-deserved reputation, but don't be afraid to try the alternatives.

Some starting points

■ A pair of hi-hats should be matched – rarely the same weight, but complementary in timbre. Often we find a heavier bottom cymbal complements a lighter top cymbal.

■ Sizes vary, but 14in is a good starting point, with both smaller and larger cymbals finding their applications. The unusual hi-hats in the picture below are 14in medium-over-heavy 'Raw', handmade by Matt Nolan of Bath.

■ The cymbals need to sound without the 'chocking' caused by air compression in a too perfect clash. To achieve this, the bottom hat needs either to simply tilt slightly via a low cymbal tilt mechanism, or to have serrated or scalloped edges to allow air to escape, as on the Custom Zildjian 'A's shown here.

■ I have even known drummers drill holes in the bottom cymbal, and Steve Gadd has rivets in these holes (though not for every gig), which is going for a different colour again.

A great ride cymbal

The 'ride' cymbal is an older member of the kit than the hi-hat, and a good-sounding ride can define a drummer. 'Good', however, is a complicated word.

The ride cymbal really came of age in the 1950s and was often large and heavy. This meant a good ride offered distinct 'stick sounds' without too many overtones. A large central 'bell' also offered a range of colours. This approach remains popular and has sometimes been called a 'ping' or a 'bounce' cymbal. Think Pete York and his fabulous early work with Steve Winwood.

In the '60s a good ride could be lighter, generating a wash of sound with many overtones to provide a cushion for the groove. Think Ringo. Sometime rivets are added to the cymbal for extra sustain and wash, called a 'sizzle' cymbal.

As PA systems improved in the '70s less wash became necessary, and the accent returned to more definition. Some rides became very heavy and the bell became smaller, its role taken by smaller 'effects' cymbals. As rock became louder the 'rock' ride evolved, often heavy and more rudely tooled for a dry loud sound with distinct individual 'notes'.

All these options are still with us, and every shade of colour in between. The challenge is to find a ride that offers both individual personality to your playing and fits the music you're playing. I'm still searching!

Cymbals: alchemy and evolution

In Asia Minor in 1200BC the goddess Cybele was worshipped to the sound of the cymbal. In the 21st century Madonna and Lady Gaga uphold that tradition.

Every drummer is at some time drawn to the ancient city of Istanbul, straddling the Bosporus where Europe becomes Asia. To this day, in the sweaty backstreets of the old city artisans are to be found at the Istanbul works, stripped to the waist, heaving solid fuel into ancient kilns and stirring vats of bronze alloy. The set alloys are then hand-hammered and lathe-trimmed to create those magical discs we all love to play.

Since 1929 a lot of that alchemy has moved to the USA, with Avedis Zildjian III setting up his works in Fayette Street, Massachusetts. This family, with a tradition dating back to 1623, remain the most prominent of traditional makers, albeit now employing very modern manufacturing systems.

Now there are at least ten great cymbal manufacturers worldwide, mostly sticking to the 'secret' formula of 80:20 bronze, as well as scores of small artisans working with everything from bronze to stainless steel.

This is a great time to buy cymbals – the traditional makers produce consistent quality and the variety available is unprecedented.

The 'crash'

We need to start with a good all-rounder that defines those accents in the groove without drawing too much attention to itself. Most drummers have opted for smaller 16–18in cymbals, generally thinner for a quick dramatic response.

Buying cymbals

■ Buy the best you can afford. Cheap cymbals will drive you crazy – they don't have character, they don't sustain and they add nothing to the music.

■ Buy in 'sets' if you can, as cymbals have to complement each other and work as one instrument, just like the drums. If you have to buy piecemeal take your existing cymbals to the shop and try them together, always with a kit. You can't judge a cymbal in isolation – it's too academic – only the sound and the blend count. This is why you should never buy cymbals on the Internet.

■ Test the whole cymbal – stick the body of the cymbal bell to the rim. Try the bell and the edge. Would it work as a crash as well as a ride? Does an upstroke also produce a useful sound? Try playing along with the muzak in the shop, does the cymbal sit with the track or jar?

■ Try your favourite stick weight, mallets and brushes – does the cymbal offer a range of useful sounds?

■ Try different dynamics, fff to ppp. Is the cymbal responding quickly enough?

■ Have someone else play the cymbals and listen from an audience perspective – does the sound carry well?

In the end, the only alchemy that matters to you as a practical musician is that which your music works on the audience, so choose your cymbals for this magic, and with your ears – not your eye on the label.

Cymbals: the infinite variety

So the basic 'groove machine' needs four cymbals. How about a long gig full of varied songs and maybe a drum solo? This is where those bronzed beauties can truly shine. Cymbals provide an infinite variety of musical colour, giving shimmer to an intro or drama to a climax. So where to begin?

Gongs & tam-tams

Just so it's clear; a 'bossed' gong has a defined pitch and a tam-tam has a wash of pitches like a cymbal, both useful in different contexts. They're often round and range from 6in to 3m, depending on how much dry ice is involved in the finale. These English tam-tams are known as 'bat heads' and offer a fantastical flourish for the end of a set.

Splash!

The humble splash cymbal started out as a comic effect in music halls and vaudeville – hitting the cymbal timed for a custard pie. The small size 6–12in and light weight makes for a fast response and short decay. Buddy Rich and Gene Krupa brought the splash from the traps kit to the modern kit and countless rock drummers have followed. I like the larger Istanbul splashes but also have smaller 'bells'.

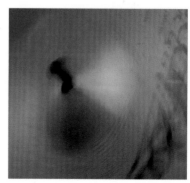

China

This piece of alchemy combines the turned-up edges of a traditional Chinese cymbal with a useful conventional bell. The China has a longer history in the kit than the Turkish cymbal and is great for those dramatic moments at the end of a big fill. The size of a China varies between 6–22in – the smaller the China, the shorter the decay. Wuhan make traditional authentic Chinas in Wuhan city and Hubei province in, yes, China.

Burnished?

As well as looking different these ride cymbals sound subtly different. Could the 22in B15 Medium Dark Matt Nolan Custom shown be the elusive perfect ride? If not, he'll make you another!

Bronzed out?

Who says all cymbals have to be bronze? This custom paper-thin crash also from Matt Nolan is honed from stainless steel and is the expensive end of 'trash'. This one really stands out from the crowd, both visually and aurally. Keep an open mind with cymbals and fit the sound to the song.

Made in Turkey?

Not any more. In the global village, cymbals are made everywhere. Istanbuls are still made by the Bosporus, but many Turkish-style cymbals are made in the USA by Avedis Zildjian of Norwell, Massachusetts. Other great marques include Paiste from Estonia (but made in Switzerland since 1957), Upif made in Italy, Sabian made by Robert Zildjian in Canada and Meinl made in Germany. Matt Nolan works from his own smithy in Bath, England, and epitomises scores of custom craftsmen across the globe.

Cymbal mounting

Mounting a cymbal may seem pretty mundane, but this apparently simple task can make a huge difference to the sound.

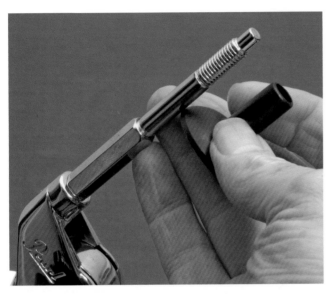

■ Generally these days we use a small plastic gizmo to protect the cymbal from the metal threads on the stand.

■ A couple of felts below the cymbal protect the underside of the bell and avoid any mechanical rattle.

■ A couple of felts above protect the bell from a top screw.

■ The top screw is usually now made of a hard plastic rather than the old metal wing nuts. This Tama screw has a useful release spring; Vater do another version called the Slick Nut.

■ Experiment with the tension on the cymbal – a loose cymbal offers a broad range of frequencies and is able to move, giving a phase shift effect to the perceived sound.

■ The extreme of this is the old-type rubber grommets that allow a splash to move very freely – precarious, but the best sound.

■ A tightly-held ride cymbal will lose some of its high frequency resonance, which may be a useful sound. Beware, however, of hard strikes on a tightly bound cymbal – the highly stressed molecules of hammered bronze can easily crack and split.

■ If a cymbal splits at the bell you can often prevent further splitting by enlarging the hole – as with this old Turkish 'K' Zildjian. Generally cracks and splits at the edge radically alter the sound of a cymbal – rarely for the better – though halting the split with a hole is worth a try. Drill by hand, and use coolant to ensure the cymbal doesn't overheat. See page 89 regarding cleaning cymbals.

Sticks, beaters, brushes and flares

An unusual tone colour provided
by a mallet or rute can really
give a lift to an intro or
a middle eight.

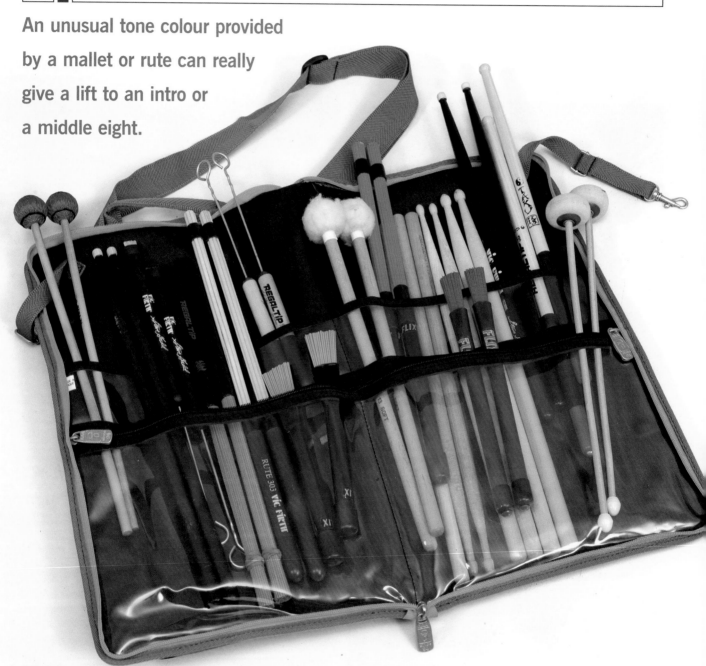

Sticks

We all have our favourite sticks, usually arrived at through
a lot of experiment. In the end we find something that feels
right and tend to stick with it; their known response becomes
a comforting factor amidst a sea of intangibles – the acoustic
of the room, the crowd, the set list ... you know the form.

Ironically, the traditional sticks many of us still use – slim

and tapered with a rounded bead – were initially developed
for military bands and are ideal for snare-drum rudiments.
However, does that remain the main focus of what kit drummers
do? Don't we spend a lot of time forging a groove between
hi-hat, ride cymbal, snare and bass? It's not surprising, then,
that radical stick designs are beginning to emerge.

Time to leave the comfort zone?

A wildly different set of sticks may give your playing a lift – something heavier will make that metal rock groove seem easy. Let the sticks do the work. Something really light, like the 7As depicted, will make that jazz middle eight swing. (**NB** For scale purposes, the laptop snare practice pad is 13in.)

■ Nylon tips started out as an erratic experiment – I remember nylon bullets flying at the crowd! – but they made cymbals sound great. Modern adhesives and manufacturing methods mean they stay intact longer now, and they come with intriguing flanges and grooves for a range of tones. Those in the picture are from the inventor Joe Calato, and are now made by Regal Tip.

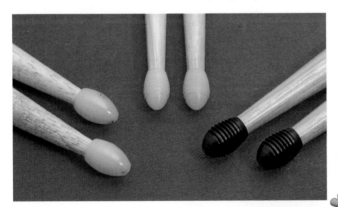

■ Felt tips such as these American Classic 5A 'soft touch' from Vic Firth are perfect for those mellow moments that don't quite fit with brushes or mallets.

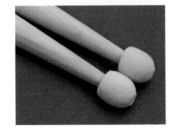

■ Virtually all sticks are made of hickory, oak or rock maple, straight-grained and tough, though lancewood and carbon fibre have their fans. Carbon fibre is very tough, but a little heavier than wood.

■ Steve Gadd has his own range of Regal Tip wooden sticks with black-painted bodies and a range of tips in wood and nylon.

■ Almost every high-profile drummer has signature sticks – these are Regal Tip Taku Hirano sticks, with rubber-coated counterweighted handles. Jeff Hamilton likes these '7A-like' jazz sticks with elongated tips.

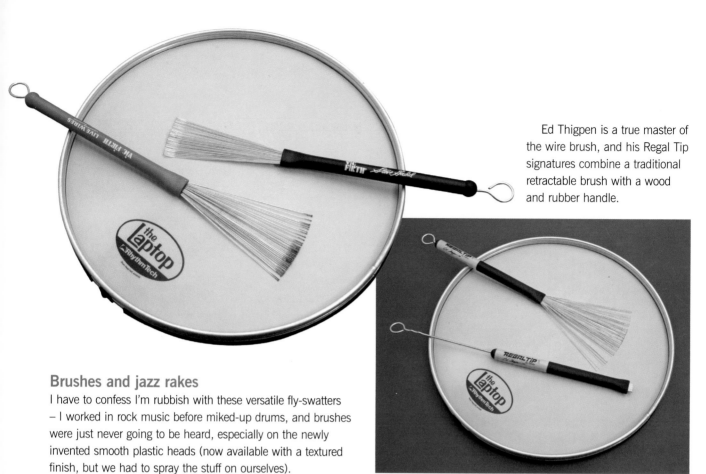

Ed Thigpen is a true master of the wire brush, and his Regal Tip signatures combine a traditional retractable brush with a wood and rubber handle.

Brushes and jazz rakes

I have to confess I'm rubbish with these versatile fly-swatters – I worked in rock music before miked-up drums, and brushes were just never going to be heard, especially on the newly invented smooth plastic heads (now available with a textured finish, but we had to spray the stuff on ourselves).

'Jelly Roll' Morton claims to have invented brushes at a gig where his drummer was playing too loud: 'Out in Los Angeles I had a drummer that hit his snares so loud that one night I gave him a couple of fly-swatters for a gag. This drummer fell in with the joke and used them, but they worked so smooth he kept right on using them. So we have "the swats" today – a nice soft way to keep your rhythm going.'

However, William Ludwig told me that New Orleans drummers had experimented with Allis and Weins 'fly-swatters' swished across calf heads, which they patented in 1913 and Ludwig issued as 'Jazz Sticks'. Drummer Vic Berton may also have had a hand in their invention.

I'm inspired to persevere by Steve Gadd's creative use of his custom brushes with upturned snag-free ends.

Vic Firth 'Live Wires' have nice beaded ends for better ride cymbal response.

On electronic kits and in loud situations the 'Jazz Rake' available from Flix offers three different gauges, light to heavy. These are the medium and heavy.

When you need a stick 'feel' but less volume, Flares from Flix, Rutes from Vic Firth or Thai Grip Fans from Regal Tip offer a range of good alternatives.

Steve Gadd sometimes uses Samba drumsticks on his kit for that authentic Brazilian crack, and I have a fabulous pair of Rattle Stix from Remo which will one day be invaluable – they combine a mallet with a shaker.

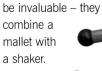

Mallets and beaters

Many drummers have used timpani beaters, and I've had these Premier ones since the days of Fleetwood Mac's *Albatross*. They have a useful plastic bead at the other end. Foote's softer lambswool 13s come in handy for timpani impressions, and these much harder Vic Firth M10s have occasional uses.

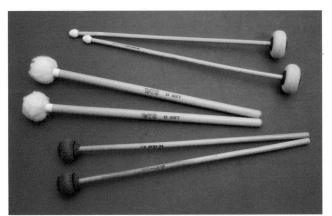

A good stick bag

A well-organised stick bag keeps everything to hand, and if attached to a tom makes for easy access during a gig. If you're concerned about damping the tom too much then the stick bag could just as easily attach to a music stand. These clear plastic Protection Racket types make it easier to see what sticks are available.

A stick holder

You know the scenario – that pair of mallets you positioned carefully ready for the break in the middle of the song but now on the floor under the big tom? A stick holder may be a good purchase if you go for a lot of changes or are prone to breakages. This one is from Vater and comes in different sizes, with a versatile stand clamp and drum-key adjustable angle brace.

Gloves

Did you ever look at the snare and wonder whose blood you could see sprayed on the batter head, then realise it's yours? I've often cut my hands on the hi-hat without even realising, so maybe drummers' gloves aren't just for wimps. These Vater types are meshed for cool running.

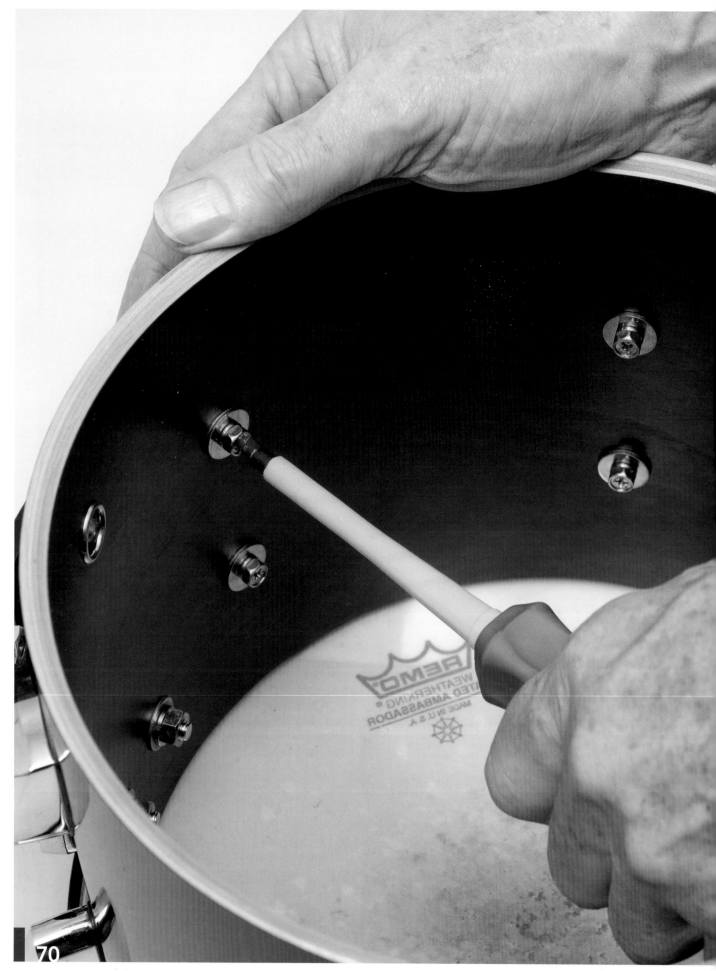

Improving your kit's performance

The drum set has gone from organic log and skin to a mechanical groove machine in 100 short years. But that machine needs lubrication and servicing to keep it cooking on the back beat and thus free-up the energy and imagination of the player.

As drummers, we all have that nagging feeling that somehow we could get more from our kit. Should we try better heads or different heads? Would new or radical sticks do it? Or should we clean those ageing cymbals? Is that new gizmo really going to help our bass drum kick the back of the stalls? Well, the answers to all these questions and more can be found on the next few pages.

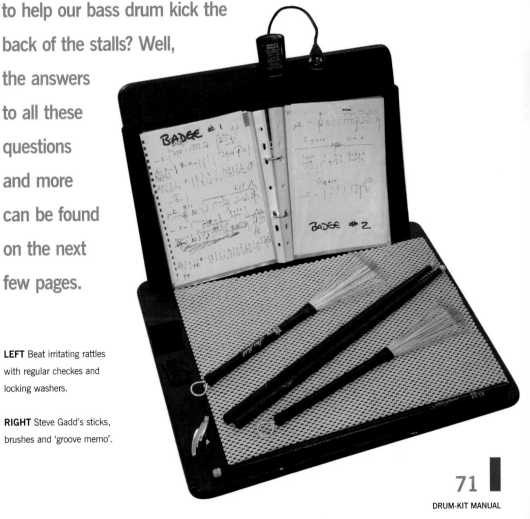

LEFT Beat irritating rattles with regular checkes and locking washers.

RIGHT Steve Gadd's sticks, brushes and 'groove memo'.

Safety first

Generally speaking working on your drum kit should not cause undue risk. However, there are some hazards of which you should be aware.

Electric shock: electronic kits & stage monitors

Sadly some electric kit players have been injured through accidental exposure to mains current. Though the UK's adoption of 240V may seem to present a greater risk than the USA's 110V, it's actually the amperes that are the killer not the volts! Amperes are the measure of current, and high currents are the ones to avoid.

Drum monitor amplifiers run happily on domestic supplies at relatively low current ratings, so the situation of one player one amp is a pretty safe scenario, especially if we observe a few precautions:

■ Always ensure a good earth or ground connection. This allows a safe path to earth for any stray current, which always flows along the easiest path. The earth or ground offers a quicker route to earth than through you, and therein lies its safety potential.
■ Never replace fuses with the wrong value eg a 5-amp fuse in a 3-amp socket. Fuses are there to protect us and our equipment from power surges. A higher value means less protection. Never replace a fuse with a bodge such as silver foil or similar. This offers no protection at all.
■ Consider using an earth leakage trip or similar circuit-breaker in any situation where you have no control or knowledge of the mains power.
■ Maintain any mains leads. Check them regularly for damage and strained wires. If fitted the earth wire *must* be in place.
■ Never operate an amplifier with the safety cover removed, especially valve amplifiers known for their HT circuits.
■ Never put drinks on or near amplifiers.
■ Never touch a stage lighting circuit or lamp. Apart from mains electricity issues they're often also dangerously hot. Leave stage lamps to qualified electricians.

Beware of

■ Multi amp/multi PA scenarios that aren't professionally administered. Professional PA and lighting supervisors are very safety-conscious and trained in health and safety to a legal minimum requirement. The danger comes with 'semi pro' and amateur rigs which aren't closely scrutinised. If you're in any doubt don't plug in until you've talked to the on-site supervisor and feel you can trust his assurances.

■ Unknown stage situations, especially those that feature big lighting rigs. This is easily said but hard to adhere to. Even the most modest gigs nowadays have quite sophisticated lights and sound. The crucial issue is that all the audio equipment is connected to the same PHASE. Danger particularly arises when microphones are connected to one PHASE and monitors to another. A drummer/vocalist could find himself as the 'bridge' between 30 amps of current! If in any doubt be rude and ask.

Hearing damage

Acoustic drummers in the Jazz age had little fear of hearing damage – though big bands with full brass sections can emit peaks well over 100dB. The real problems arose with amplification; Leo Fender's first amplifier knocked out a feverish 3W of audio; by the early '60s The Beatles had a 30W amp each, and Paul McCartney had a T60. By 1964 The Beatles had the first 100W VOX amps, specifically made to cope with concerts in vast football stadiums and the noise of immense screaming crowds.

By 1970 100W was the norm for a guitar 'head' in a small club and the first 10,000W PA systems had rocked Woodstock.

Pete Townshend of The Who first complained of the hearing impairment tinnitus in the mid-'70s and for many years refused to tour with a band as his hearing worsened. Drummers are even more at risk due to the transient peaks induced by a snare rimshot trying to match a 200 watt guitar amplifier.

The key to saving your hearing is 'dose' figures. Research has shown that you risk damage if exposed to sound 'dose' levels of 90dB or above for extended periods. Health and safety limits for recording studios now recommend no more than 90dBA ('A' standing for average) per eight-hour day, these levels to be reduced dramatically if the period is longer or the dBA higher.

Transient peaks, as in those produced by a loud snare drum or hi-hat, can easily push levels beyond these figures. Be careful where you sit in relation to your drums and monitors – a small movement can effect a dramatic change in transient sound level. Don't be afraid to ask about peak and average levels. Your ears are your greatest asset as a musician, so don't be embarrassed in to thinking you can't question sound levels.

Chemical hazards

Paints and solvents

Traditionally some drums were painted with nitrocellulose lacquer but this practice is now rare. Nitrocellulose lacquers produce a very hard yet flexible, durable finish that can be polished to a high gloss. The drawbacks of these lacquers include the hazardous nature of the solvent, which is flammable, volatile and toxic. The dangers inherent in the inhalation of spray paints are serious enough to be covered by legal statutes in the USA, UK and Europe.

Symptoms

- **Acute and chronic ingestion:** Large doses may cause nausea, narcosis, weakness, drowsiness and unconsciousness.
- **Inhalation:** irritation to nose and throat. At high concentrations, same effects as ingestion.
- **Skin:** Cracking of skin, dermatitis and secondary infections.
- **Eyes:** Irritation.
- **Symptoms of overexposure:** Repeated skin contact may cause dermatitis, while the skin defatting properties of this material may aggravate an existing dermatitis.
  (Source: Material Safety Data Sheet.)

Polyurethane

Vapours may accumulate in inadequately ventilated/confined areas. Vapours may form explosive mixtures with air. Vapours may travel long distances and flashback may occur. Closed containers may explode when exposed to extreme heat.

Symptoms

- **Ingestion:** May be similar to inhalation symptoms – drowsiness, dizziness, nausea, irritation of digestive tract, depression, aspiration hazard.

- **Inhalation:** Dizziness, drowsiness, fatigue, weakness, headache, unconsciousness.
- **Skin:** Drying, cracking, dermatitis.
- **Eyes:** Burning, tearing, reddening. Possible transient corneal injury or swelling of conjunctiva.
  (Source: Carbon Black Carcinogen by IARC, Symptoms of Overexposure.)

Recommended precautions

Always wear goggles/full face shield and other protective equipment. Avoid skin contact by wearing protective clothing. Take a shower and bathe your eyes after exposure. Wash contaminated clothing thoroughly before reusing it.

... So, with all this in mind, remember that the addresses of recommended drum repair techs and spray shops can be found in your local *Yellow Pages*.

If you really feel you want to customise your drums then you must take extreme precautions, particularly to avoid inhalation of the dangerous mist created by the spray process.

A passive mask available from DIY stores will only offer the most minimal protection. If in any doubt consult the paint manufacturer for detailed precautions specific to the paint type you've chosen.

Ear protection

There is now a huge range of ear protection available for drummers and you may want to have a custom ear insert made if you're working with your kit for long hours every day. These are expensive but you're worth it!

One manufacturer, ProGuard, offer custom earplugs that use acoustic filters developed by the acclaimed French musician and sound engineer Franck Lopez. Their built-in passive loudness filter technology allows you to hear the music with full acoustic range, whilst protecting your ears from dangerous noise levels.

The ProGuard Earsonics Pro-Musicians Custom Earplugs includes three choices of acoustic filters: 8dB (Soft Pad) low-level protection; 13dB (Medium Pad) medium-level protection, and 17dB (Hard Pad) high-level protection.

Repetitive strain injury

Drummers need to think about posture, warm-up routines and avoiding over-practising. RSI is not funny and affects millions of players. Generate good habits early and stick to them.

Tools and working facilities

Many drum kit adjustments can be done using regular domestic workshop tools. However, some specialist tools can make work such as bearing edge adjustment easier.

Necessary workshop tools

Some of the tools listed below can double up as your essential gig bag wrap, but as you don't have to carry all the workshop tools around we can be less concerned about weight and portability. It's very convenient, for instance, to have separate screwdrivers rather than the interchangeable-bit variety.

■ **Set of Phillips-type screwdrivers sizes 0, 1 and 2**
It may seem a small point but we recommend using the correct size and type of screwdriver. Many valuable instruments have survived 30 years on the road but often have a selection of odd screws and 'stripped' screw heads. These look unsightly, slow down maintenance and make the simplest job a chore. The correct 'point' size will reduce screw stripping and is also less likely to skate across your woodwork.

■ Use size 0 for some badges.
■ Use size 1 for some lugs and hardware.
■ Use size 2 for many lugs and fittings.

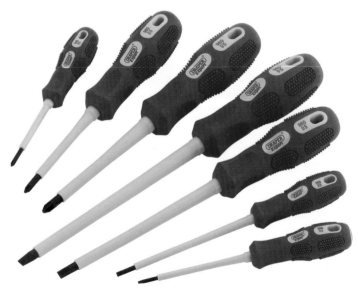

Tech Tip

When working with brittle plastic wraps consider using a fixed torque screwdriver, set to avoid over tensioning.

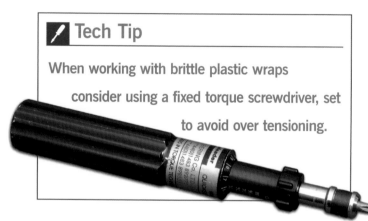

A screwdriver with interchangeable heads is an alternative option. However, you'll often need several heads at the same time, which means a lot of changing around. This option is nevertheless useful on the road, when a compact toolkit is more practical.

Sometimes an electric screwdriver can take the strain out of repetitive tasks such as removing heads, but be sure to protect the heads in case the screwdriver 'torques out'.

■ **12in (150 mm) ruler**
(with 1/32in and 1/64in increments) (0.5 mm increments).

■ **Substantial pliers**
Put tape on the claws for chrome protection.

■ **Straight edge**
For checking snare beds.

■ **4mm straight-slot screwdriver**
Useful for many applications.

■ **Portable suction fixing vice**
This ingenious device is terrific if you have no suitable permanent workbench.

■ **Screw extractor HSS drills and tap wrenches** For removing broken screws.

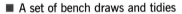

■ **Evans or DW electric screwdriver attachment**
Makes light work of head changes.

■ **Drum keys**
One size doesn't quite fit all, especially vintage drums which require a slotted key. The picture shows a Premier 1960s type.

■ **A set of bench draws and tidies**
For all those often misplaced odds and sods that are essential for drum maintenance.

■ **Electronic tuner**
An accurate electronic tuner such as the Drum Tuna makes for consistent tensioning. Alternatives are the Neary Drum Torque or the Rhythm Tech Protorq, which measure consistent bolt torque.

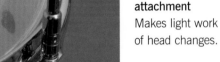

■ **Polish and cloth**
A soft duster for drum shells and cymbals, preferably lint free. Proprietary drum polishes differ from household furniture polishes, which often contain silicone. The wax used in drum polish is emulsified to avoid any sticky residue, especially under the heat from stage lighting. See page 88.

■ **Soldering Iron**
For electric kit repairs. This should be at least 25W with a penlight tip. The iron is essential when repairing electrical wiring. It's worth investing in a stand with a sponge cleaner attached. A crocodile clip multi-arm is also useful for holding small components in place.

■ **A tube of solder**
Multicore-type non-acid resin.

■ **A small penlite torch**
Useful for closer examination of details. Useful any time but especially in a stageside emergency.

In addition all the drum techs and cymbal makers consulted for this book seemed to have their own ingenious home-made tools for very specific jobs.

Useful accessories

- Hole cutter for 'O' ports.
- Lug lube or Vaseline or ChapStick for thread lubrication.
- An old electric toothbrush is useful for cleaning cymbal tone grooves.
- Protractor, for determining accuracy of bearing edges.

- An electronic multimeter for testing electro kit circuits and wiring looms.
- A set of socket spanners – good for removing and tightening lugs and some hardware.
- Loctite or similar multi-purpose superglue.
- A craft knife/penknife has multiple uses, such as snare stringing etc.
- Thread gauges, useful for checking for correct threads on replacement screws etc.
- Wire stripper for electrical repairs.

Working environment

Many drum repairs and much maintenance can be safely carried out with the drum resting on a normal kitchen table or on a Workmate-type DIY bench, suitably padded. The photographs in this book were 80% done at home on a Draper Workmate. However, see page 73 on paint repairs for precautions regarding inhalation of cellulose etc.

A small 1m square of carpet sample blue tacked to a workbench can avoid a lot of inadvertent damage to drum finishes and paintwork.

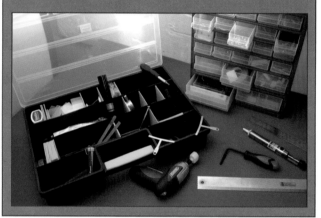

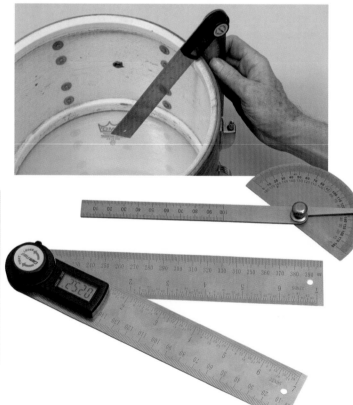

Essential gig bag accessories

Carrying a few spares can save you a long walk, but you have enough to carry to a gig without hauling your whole toolkit around. The mere essentials compactly stowed will potentially save a lot of pre-gig hassle, and this Protection Racket bag should fit in the side compartment of your cymbal-bag.

We suggest...

- A multipoint screwdriver with Phillips 0, 1 and 2 bits and small and medium point conventional straight heads. A straight-slot screwdriver is useful to have around for dealing with broken mains plugs and blown fuses.
- A small pair of wire snips plus spare nylon string for emergency snare wire changes.
- A few spare felts and a plastic sleeve – they vanish!
- An electronic Drum Tuna or similar.
- Spare snare head. (OK, not in the gig bag!)
- A penlight torch.
- A Leatherman or similar multitool – useful for a sharp blade and decent pliers.
- Allen or hex keys if your gear uses them.
- Two drum keys.
- Small 'emergency only' soldering iron and 6in of solder if you have any piezo triggers or Roland stuff.
- Some 13-amp and 5-amp (UK) fuses as well as any specific to your area of touring (ie USA and European equivalents, etc).
- Insulating tape.
- Spare pedal spring.

Vater and others do a handy 'tech pack' containing most of the spares you're likely to need and are likely to mislay.

Unfortunately, by having this kit with you you'll acquire a reputation as Mr Ever Ready, and before long everybody in the band will come to depend on your tools!

It's worth doing a little maintenance

…Or getting an expert to do it for you. A drum kit may look rugged but that's an illusion, and shells and hardware are easily broken. However, even the rigours of the world tour have been surmounted with the help of some good flight cases and a little loving care. Clearly few of us would risk taking a vintage Gretsch on the road, but barring abuse and given a few careful tweaks it would undoubtedly acquit itself well. The Premier '64 and the Gene Krupa Slingerland in our case studies are still being gigged.

Vintage antiques

If you're lucky enough to own a vintage kit then what you have in your possession is not just a good instrument but a piece of popular music history. Given its rarity, you must regard the kit as you would any other valuable 'antique'.

Whilst such drums are starting to be considered a valuable investment, I personally share the view of many antique furniture collectors that design and function are part of the charm of such items and therefore they're best kept in use. I wonder about the 'investor' who thinks an instrument is best consigned to a bank vault. For me this seems a waste, like the owner who never actually drives his Ferrari. Researching in the world's museums I've observed that unplayed instruments simply wilt and die.

So I recommend you enjoy your kit whilst observing a few precautions:

- Never subject drums and cymbals to any extreme changes in temperature and humidity. The chief victim here is the finish, which can crack or 'pave' as the underlying wood shrinks or expands. Vintage drums are more prone to this as their paints and glazes may be pervious – which may contribute to the character of their sound as the wood continues to 'breathe'. Protect glitters and sparkle wraps from direct sunlight, as UV causes discolouration and fading.
- Give the drums, cymbals and hardware a good wipe down with a lint-free cloth after playing. This will reduce any damage to metal parts and finish caused by perspiration – the main cause of rust to the rims and lugs.
- Keep all the moving parts suitably lubricated, especially threads.

Authenticity

Many true 'relics' of the last 100 years have defective parts, particularly threads. It's perfectly natural to want to replace these. However, it's almost a custodial responsibility to replace these tastefully. These drums will outlive us and carry on being worthwhile instruments for centuries. I predict the authentic 'early music' enthusiasts of 2050 will include people performing Beatles grooves on authentic Ludwig Downbeats. So seek out the most authentic replacement parts possible. It's possible to buy genuine parts with a suitable patina that ooze an atmosphere of smoky bars and long years on the chitlin circuit (see *Useful contacts* appendix). Do, however, make a careful note of any changes, as this will save argument over authenticity at a later date.

■ Keep the original parts

Authenticity remains an issue 'under the hood', and with an old instrument it's extremely prudent to conserve any original bits. This may sound over the top at present but the collectors and players of the next century will remember you warmly for taking that extra bit of trouble.

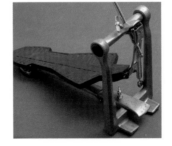

Over the years I've personally accumulated a small collection of bits from previous kits, including a couple of stands and pedals from my first proper Olympic kit. Now in 1966 when I sold the kit, these seemed to be scrap metal and it never occurred to me to pass these on. But if the kit still exists then these those old parts are an important part of what antiquarians call 'provenance'. A dealer may spot the replacement stands I obtained with great difficulty in 1966 and wonder if the kit really is a '64 Red Sparkle, but if the present owner has the old parts it completes a part of that story which supports the authenticity of the overall instrument.

So put those old parts in a safe place and label them with any information you have.

When not to re-finish

Never be tempted to respray or re-cover a vintage Gretsch. However tatty it may have become *it's probably worth more in its original state*. Again it's like the 'bruises' on a piece of Chippendale furniture – they're a testimony to the artefact's history. The same, of course, applies to younger kits, but somehow they don't resonate with quite the same history (yet!).

Do-it-yourself versus calling in an expert

We all have varying levels of competency in carpentry and painting. I personally made some silly mistakes as a teenager, and this book is part driven by the desire to help others avoid my youthful errors.

So bottom line is, if you're good with tools and prepared to be diligent and extremely careful, you can probably do most of what this manual expounds and either maintain a lovely instrument in peak performance or radically improve a budget Pearl. However, if you have *any doubt at all* about your abilities call an expert.

Today there are at least three skilled drum techs in every major city in the world and they all have a sneaking regard for the old warhorses that keeps bouncing back.

Never

■ Practise refinishing on a vintage instrument. Buy a budget drum and learn the craft first.
■ Attempt a respray unless you have all the required tools and skills and a dust-free environment. Always wear a protective mask and protective clothing.
■ Force the wrong size screw in a shell or component. Consider using fixed torque screwdrivers on vintage instruments.
■ Always protect the drum shells during any maintenance or lubrication.

But whatever else you do, enjoy that special piece of popular music history by playing it every day and trying very hard to wear it out!

I have seen and played a lot of drums in the last 50 years and I have this thought to pass on:

A well set-up budget Yamaha is a better working instrument than a poorly set-up custom order DW. In crude terms a good working kit is about 70% set-up and 20% the synergy of the parts – all pieces of wood are different and even machined metal parts vary in their composition and microscopic detail. The last 10% is alchemy. A good drum is a good drum whether old or new. As my late great teacher Brendan John McCormack often said, 'It's just a plank of wood – *you* have to make the music!'

Does a kit respond to being played well? Does the prevalent temperature and humidity affect a drum's sound? Yes. But *great kits* still have a certain mystery about them – long may it remain.

Stageside repairs

Get to the gig as early as possible and check your kit is all working.
Drum-kits take a bit of a hammering and things do go wrong!

■ **Oh hell, we're being introduced by the MC and I've just trashed the snare head!**
Typical snare head change and settle? Ten minutes, if you carry a spare head! Carry a spare snare? This may sound outrageous, but try and do a gig without one. So I seriously suggest you buy a second contrasting snare – a piccolo or tenor. You'll love it, so it may end up permanently on the stand!

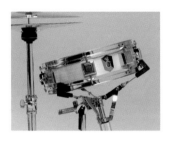

■ **My cymbal stand has developed brewers' droop!**
Gaffer tape! No drummer should travel without gaffer tape. Jam or lash the offending hardware – it will probably hold for one gig.

■ **I've stripped a thread on a tension bolt or hardware!**
PTFE plumbers' tape may temporarily hold a stripped thread. Replace properly ASAP.

■ **I've broken one of my favourite lucky sticks!**
'Always buy at least two pairs of your favourite sticks. That way you have to break three before you hit a crisis.' – Des Dyer.

■ **My snare wires have caught in the trap case and are stretched out of shape!**
Most standard snare wires are attached with nylon string or a strip of mylar, but a trimmed piece of discarded drum head makes a useful substitute in an emergency. Alternatively, Puresound offer a 'speed mount' system using a simple cotter pin through a fabric snare tie, which saves a little time untying and retying strings or undoing friction clamps when a gig is imminent.

Heads you win!

My first drums were rope-tensioned with calf heads and the snare was made of catgut strands. They sounded great but were frail, and certainly not rock'n'roll.

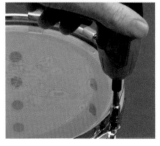

As the '50s turned to the '60s I acquired a bolt-tensioned kit, but the calf heads remained. These broke at the first shout of *Twist and Shout*. Every second week I would be down at Liverpool's Rushworth's music store grovelling to the nice man in the suit behind the counter – please could he re-lap my heads this week (three days minimum, and each drum had its own eccentric-sized hoop – 13.75in wasn't unusual).

If you lived in the USA, Marion 'Chick' Evans in 1956 and innovative banjo-head manufacturer Remo Belli saved your bacon in 1957 with their 'plastic' heads, developed from experiments with Bo PET (biaxially-oriented polyethylene terephthalate), a polyester film made from stretched polyethylene terephthalate.

In Liverpool we had to wait, though Premier's Everplay Extras did apparently also appear in London in 1957.

Internationally the most well-known trade names for these mylar and melinex and hostaphan heads are Remo, Evans and Aquarian, though there are many other makers, and all vary the formula to achieve different base materials. Originally Remo's 'Weatherkings' were white and opaque to help mimic the look of calfskin. Later innovations included clear drumheads, two-ply drumheads (for added durability and depth) and simulated natural drumheads using a product called 'Fiberskyn', which is currently in its third version.

A different head can change the sound of any drum dramatically, so I recommend you experiment until you find the sound you're looking for. This may take your whole life, but celebrate that! The major manufacturers offer scores of variations and the following are just some of what's available.

■ Single-ply mylar

These heads have been the staple of drumming for the last 60 years. They have a lot of highs and often need taming with some form of damping in order to bring out the fundamental of the drum, but they're reliable and rugged. Coated versions are good for wire bushes and carry an inbuilt damping factor. These heads are commonly used on snares – batter and resonant, the resonant usually 'clear'. Different weights also sound different; generally heavier, thicker heads are less prone to high frequency overtones. The picture shows a 10mm clear.

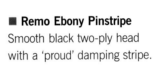

■ Double-ply

Popular from the late '70s on for their muted high frequency response, which emphasises the fundamental, these are great for heavy rock. They're often 'oil-filled', with a distinctive oil-slick rainbow appearance. This is an Evans G2 version 7mm double-ply with no pinstripe, designed for toms.

■ Hazy snare

A not quite so clear snare resonant, 3mm.

■ Power dot

Aquarian have a patent on this type of single-ply head with a centre spot for a focused emphasis on the fundamental. This one is coated for snare brushwork.

■ Reverse dot

As the name suggests, this head combines a tone ring and a centre spot, both mounted on the inside of the head. Single 7mm and double 14mm versions are available.

■ Remo Suede Emperor

Two free-floating plies of 7.5mm mylar film, which offer open warm tones with enhanced durability. Has a slight texture.

■ Remo Ebony Pinstripe

Smooth black two-ply head with a 'proud' damping stripe.

■ Fiberskyn 3

A retro head echoing the character of calf but with the durability of plastics.

■ Calf

Still available, and essential for older drums with their non-standard hoop sizes. You retain your personal hoop and drum techs such as Eddie Ryan will make you a real 'skin' to order.

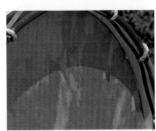

■ Evans EC Resonant Clear

A resonant with an inbuilt internal metallic damping ring.

Bass drum heads

Controlling bass drum resonance for clarity and definition has been an issue since drummers pushed beyond single accents and 'on' beats in the 1920s. Some approaches to this issue are covered on pages 41–49. However, some modern heads now take damping on board at source.

■ Evans EQ2
This double-ply head has a double-vented tone ring.

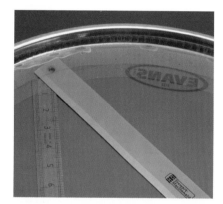

■ Evans EMAD 2
This two-ply batter has a choice of different-width interchangeable foam damping rings. A single-ply GMAD version is also available in 14mm weight.

The straight EMAD resonant version has a tone ring and a substantially reinforced 4in vent.

■ Remo Powerstroke
Clear bass drum head with tone ring second ply and double stripe.

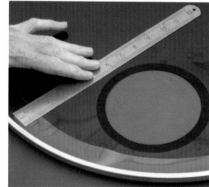

■ Evans Onyx
This matt-fronted version has an inbuilt second-ply tone ring damper and is supplied ready ported.

■ Evans Prepak sets
Many manufacturers offer pre-packed sets of heads at a discount. Changing heads as a set makes sense, but not the day before an important gig!

The above survey merely scratches the surface of the hundreds of head options currently available, so experiment – but I would respectfully suggest that you think in sets, particularly with toms. It comes back to the idea of making a kit work as one internally complementary instrument, and heads are decisive in this.

Three-monthly checks

A little light maintenance will keep your kit sounding and looking good. Most of the work below is compatible with a change of heads and worth doing at least annually, and more frequently if you're gigging heavily.

Under the heads

■ Bolts

It's worth checking the tension-bolt threads, which are prone to attracting dust and grit, making accurate tensioning more arduous. Give these a clean with some mild detergent, thoroughly dry and then relubricate with a dab of Vaseline or LP Lug Lube. 3-in-One oil (sewing machine oil) can also be applied sparingly to the lower threads of the tension rod. Do *not* use WD-40 as a lubricant, as it will remove old lubricant and then quickly evaporate – effective, though, for cleaning!

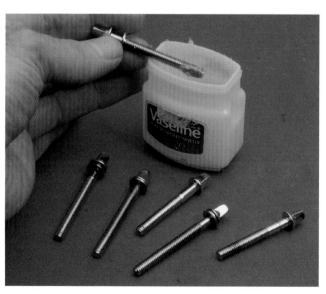

■ Lugs

Whilst you have the tools out it's worth tightening the lug screws. Note the spring washer keeping the screws tight and the large plain washer protecting the shell itself. On this kit this requires a No1 Phillips for the back screws.

Do not *overtighten* – just enough to stop the lugs moving in normal use. All the lug fittings were loose here, but not enough to cause problems yet. This is normal on many new kits due to wood shrinkage.

John Good of DW on bearing edge angles

If you look at a drum head, the more space there is under the head the more you're going to shock the drum. If you take the bearing edge angle down you allow more overtones to develop under the head. For the snare you want the shock, but for the bass drum you need a nice defined fundamental. Hence different bearing edges bring out the different qualities, sustains, attacks and resonances. I took a lot of time cutting everybody's bearing edges in Los Angeles. I used to have some really gorgeous drums from various drum companies – they had beautiful finishes but I found out that bearing edges just made such a difference, and that it was so important to tune the drum head to the fundamental of the shell to get the best out of it.

Bearing edges

Check the bearing edges for cracks in the shell or bearing-edge deformities. Any lumps and bumps will make even tensioning a chore.

In scientific terms energy transferred from the bearing edge of the drum shell and drumhead is called the 'event horizon'. When you strike the head with the stick the head vibrates and passes the kinetic energy to the wooden drum shell via the bearing edge, and the whole drum vibrates in sympathy. Any errors at the bearing edge cause chaos in the acoustic system and unpredictable results.

Accurate bearing-edge work is really about the right tools and a lot of experience, so you may want to refer any radical work to a drum tech. See page 106 for more advice in this area.

If the bearing edge is smooth and level take a candle and gently rub a bit of wax around the edges to help smooth the movement of the head over the edge. Always ensure that any lumps of wax are removed before refitting the head.

Snare strainer

On snare drums always check that the snare strainer throw-off assembly is lubricated and working smoothly. Everything here tends to work loose, so give all fixing screws a good tighten.

Also check the snares themselves for damage or bending. Replace any bent wires or frayed retaining film or string.

Hardware

A little chrome polish once in a while not only makes your stands look better but aids smooth assembly, saving time and effort. There are a number of commercial metal polishes that work well.

Not only will polish keep your stand in a pristine condition but it also seals them with a moisture-resistant coating – useful when you consider the moisture they encounter at a sweaty gig.

A snare strip-down and thorough clean

Every few years you should treat your drums to a thorough clean, which is easiest done during a strip-down. This vintage drum has been neglected!

1 Remove the heads, first taking the tension off the hoops slowly and evenly with a manual key, after which a screwdriver-mounted drum key can save time and RSI. In this case I'm using a flat-head screwdriver bit.

2 Keep all bolts and washers together in a small container.

3 Remove tone-damping dust and drumstick flakes with a vacuum.

4 It's worth removing all the fittings for a thorough cleaning. The lug retainers on many drums are No1 Phillips, and this right-angle screwdriver helps in reaching awkward spots. Take photos of what goes where in case you lose track!

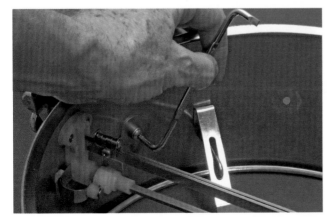

Chrome

Chrome is found all over a drum kit and can be ruined by moisture, so keeping your equipment dry is important. You should wipe down the chrome with an old terry cloth towel after every gig. If you play somewhere cool or move your equipment from a cold car to a warm club condensation will form on the metal parts. This should be wiped away immediately to prevent rust.

■ Chrome cleaners seem to work fine and also help keep the chrome protected. I've often used Silvo Tarnish Guard, with little ill effect over 50 years – the wadding is less messy than the liquid type.

■ The finished lugs and shell look very good for their age.

■ If dirt, pitting or rust builds up, you could *carefully* use 0000 grade steel wool – but be aware that re-chroming is an expensive process, so go

easy! For severe rust on unexposed parts 0 grade steel wool soaked in gasoline or naphtha will cut through. A metal polish such as DuraGlit or Noxon can be used on most metal surfaces, *excluding cymbals*.

Polish

There are polishes on the market that are specifically designed for drum-set shells. The Groove Juice 'shell shine' stuff does, however, contain silicones, so beware. This is a simple 'spray and wipe off' procedure.

The Vater brand contains carnauba and claims to be safe for plastic wraps and lacquers. It's best to apply the polish to a cloth first, not directly onto the shell. This reduces smearing.

ABOVE Groove Juice gives a good finish to these Pearl shells.

Plastic wrap finishes

For dirt and dust, simple dishwashing or hand-washing soap and warm water will suffice. Windex and other ammonia-based cleaners tend to leave the finish a bit dull. Don't use anything abrasive such as steel wool, scouring pads or abrasive cleaners like Soft Scrub. They'll naturally scratch the plastic. Avoid getting water in the lugs and threads!

Lacquered finishes

Again, warm soapy water works best to clean off dirt or other gross build-up. Pledge and similar furniture polishes work well in keeping drums shiny but may contain polymers. Guitar polish by Gibson, Fender and Martin also helps to shine them up, and have the advantage of *not* containing polymers, which can react badly to heat from stage lighting. Don't use any abrasive cleaners.

Cymbals

Cleaning cymbals is a delicate process. Note the particularly exceptional situation with the Paiste cymbals highlighted below. Modern cymbals have a protective coating that will deter oxidisation for many years. So:

■ Avoid touching the playing surfaces and hold the cymbals by the edges when mounting.

■ Dry the cymbals with a soft lint-free cloth after every playing. This helps avoid perspiration acid eating into the bronze.

As a last resort, with badly oxidised cymbals you could try a proprietary cleaner such as

Groove Juice. Be aware, however, that the solution may remove the manufacturing logo on your cymbals, and will certainly remove the protective coating. It *will* change the sound.

It's important that you don rubber gloves, as Groove Juice contains organic acids, detergents and poly solv EB (bathroom cleaner). This can cause skin burns.

Paiste

If you have Paiste cymbals, only use soapy water or Paiste brand cymbal cleaner. Paiste cymbals are surface-coated, and any other cleaning methods can cause permanent damage.

Don't use Brasso, abrasive cleaners or steel wool on any cymbal. It's better to have a dirty cymbal than a ruined one.

It's considered sacrilege to clean an old 'K' Zildjian.

1 Spray a little Groove Juice evenly on one side of the cymbal.

2 Allow 30 seconds for the juice to loosen the dirt.

3 Rinse off thoroughly with clean warm water. Towel dry.

4 Heavily soiled cymbals may respond to a light brush in the tonal grooves with an old electric toothbrush. Repeat for the rear of the cymbal.

The results are interesting. The best analogy I can find is to guitar strings – many players like the bright responsive tone of new bronze; others loathe that same brightness. I personally prefer the cleaned sound, with more high harmonics.

RIMS (Resonance Isolation Mounting System): a retro fit

Drummers have often puzzled over the different sound of a conventionally mounted tom. Gary Gauger says: 'I knew the problem existed when I bought my first drum kit in 1959. Removing the tom from the mount resulted in a fuller more sustained sound. When it was replaced, the sound was "choked" or "dead". I realised that most of the drum resonance was lost. Eventually, as a professional musician involved in recording, my goal became to recapture the resonance my drums were losing.'

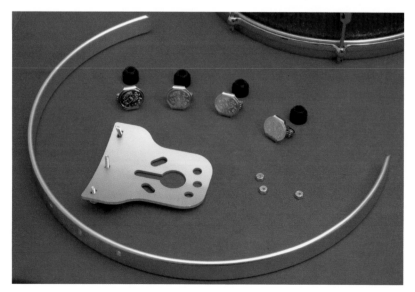

In 1979, after many experiments with different methods of mounting drums, the RIMS (Resonance Isolation Mounting System) concept was born in 1980, along with Gary's company GPI.

Most major drum manufacturers now offer a version of Gary's RIMS isolation mounts for toms. Gary himself has recently opted to use alloy mounts rather than steel, as they're less prone to intrinsic resonance and are more malleable.

Here we take a look at a retro-fit procedure on a vintage tom.

1 Attach the universal adaptor plate to the alloy RIMS band with three carriage bolts, using a 3/8in wrench.

2 Loosen the retaining screws with a No 2 Phillips and then slide the adjustable flanges on to the alloy band.

3 We will need four flanges (two per side) for a 14in tom.

4 With the top head removed, align the flanges with the drum's tension bolts and fix in place with the No 2 Phillips.

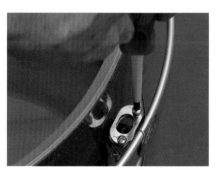

5 Add the rubber grommets and thread the drum bolts through into the flanges.

6 Check for tension in the alloy band and if necessary gently adjust the radius to remove any excess tension – it's essential that no tension is introduced on to the shell.

Bottom line

Does the drum sound better mounted like this? Yes! It sounds better than it has for the last 46 years, so much so that I'm considering using the mounts permanently, despite their unauthentic look for a vintage kit.

Pedal maintenance

As a gigging drummer your pedals take a hammering – maybe 10,000 operations per night. Smooth moving parts feel better and respond noticeably quicker; less gets in the way of the music. The bass drum and hi-hat pedals are both intensely mechanical and need a bit a of simple TLC every few months.

Lubrication

Anywhere that metal to metal friction occurs needs a tiny bit of lube. Vaseline should do the job, applied with a cocktail stick, though Gibraltar offer a dedicated pedal lube. However, don't overdue lubrication, as grease gets everywhere and attracts dust. Hinges also need sparing lube. **NB** Leave 'sealed unit' bearings alone as they're usually lifetime lubricated, and opening them up introduces grit and dust.

Chain drives

Chain lubricant (available from motorcycle or mountain bike shops) is best here, though simple WD-40 will initially expel moisture and prevent rust.

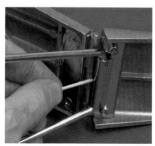

Synthetic strapping

This is sometimes leather on older pedals. Carry out a quick check for fraying and cracking, and if necessary replace before it lets you down mid-gig.

Springs

The springs are elastic and as such wear out. So if your pedal feels sluggish give it a treat – new springs are inexpensive and easy to fit. Ideally you should replace with the exact same size and torsion, though if this proves difficult there's usually enough adjustment in the tension mechanism to compensate. Lubricate the new parts at point of contact. On this Pearl:

1 Remove the old spring with a gentle prise on the spring loop. Note the old Pearl spring has a sliver of cymbal felt inserted to stop the spring squeaking – worth copying!

2 Position the replacement. Gibraltar supply their springs complete with triangle rod, which saves a lot of fiddling about.

3 Adjust the tension to suit your required 'feel' and secure.

Other checks

■ Tighten any loose nuts against their spring washers.

■ Sharpen any floor spurs with a metal file.

2 Tighten all the fixed components, as these tend to loosen due to vibration. This Pearl requires a 2.5mm Allen wrench.

3 Check the tilt mechanism and lightly lubricate.

4 Remove fluff and dirt from any Velcro grippers.

5 Check all felts and rubbers are intact.

6 Sharpen any floor spurs with a metal file.

Double pedals

On double pedals such as this Yamaha check all the linkage bearings are moving freely and lubricate sparingly.

Hi-hat maintenance

1 Lubricate the chain drive or metal linkage and any hinges.

Drum mats and marking up

As a working drummer my most difficult teenage gig was at Liverpool's Pyramid club in the 1960s. Believe it or not the stage and dance floor were all coloured glass, illuminated from below. This looked very groovy but wasn't compatible with the steel spurs and bass-drum anchors of 1965 – I was soon drumming amidst the dancers. Great fun, but not good for the essential groove.

LEFT The DW velcro, combined with a Protection Racket mat, is very effective.

Fortunately heavier kits, substantial rubber feet and over-engineered hardware have coincided with the idea of the simple drum mat. At its best this is much more than a square of old carpet found at the local carpet warehouse.

The Protection Racket mat and markers illustrated are the right size and shape for a standard kit and are 'stage presentable' and rugged, and the carpet surface above and below is non-slip and Velcro-friendly. The Velcro bit is very good news if your bass-drum pedal and hi-hat pedal have Velcro bases. If they don't you can easily fit your own using self-adhesive Velcro. Then those components will stay just where you put them.

LEFT A Protection Racket gig-friendly drum mat.

Sound protection

Many drum manufacturers now supply wooden bass drum hoops with built-in protection. If, however, you have an older kit then you can save a lot of damage and secure a better grip with these self-adhesive Gibraltar rubber hoop guards – less hassle and much better than a tatty beer mat!

Quick set-ups

If you're a gigging drummer with ten minutes to set up, then marking up your mat saves a lot of time. In the bad old days this involved lots of messy gaffer tape and scribbled notes.

The neat and pro solution involves fitting numbered Velcro hoops around your stand feet and corresponding numbers on the bases of stands – magic! Additional shaped markers for pedals, tom legs and throne tripods make speed-setting a breeze. The whole lot stays on the mat when you roll it up and move to the next gig.

Tom and snare clash?

These simple push-fit Gibraltar rubber 'drum bumpers' are especially useful in recording, where the sound of metal rims and hoops clashing is a distraction. They also help avoid damage.

Some approaches to recording drums

So your kit sounds great on stage – but will it record well? I spent 17 enjoyable years of my working life as a professional sound engineer and producer, with the benefit of a drummer's perspective.

These two 'omnis' and a D112 for the bass drum can be very effective.

Background

The great drum sound we now associate with all pop and rock recordings only really developed from about 1960. Listen to Tony Meehan's Abbey Road recordings from this period and what you hear is a great kit played well in a good room with great microphones. The sound engineering is characterised by very simple microphone techniques – a quality overhead microphone for the kit and a big dynamic mike for the bass drum, all of this recorded simply though a valve-driven mixer with little or no EQ or compression.

The Beatles recordings at Abbey Road in 1962–66 applied

this approach, and it can still produce good results *if* the kit itself sounds great. Drummer Uriel Jones asserts that many early '60s Motown hits were made with one drum mike!

Unfortunately, for a number of reasons many kits of that era didn't sound great at source, and engineers and producers strived for years to counteract this by manufacturing sounds in the studio from what was available. To do this, more and more microphones were used, ever closer to individual drums and cymbals.

A typical rig

■ Two snare mikes, top and bottom, positioned very close to the heads – often Shure Unidynes or similar hyper-cardioid dynamic mikes.

NB If you try this the resonant head microphone often needs to be set at the mixing desk to the opposite phase to the batter head, to avoid cancellation effects.

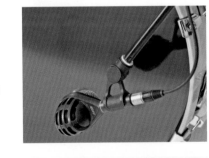

■ A bass drum mike, often a large diaphragm dynamic such as the AKG D112 literally *in* the bass drum.

■ If there's no port in the resonant head for microphone access then an external approach can also work, though definition can be harder to achieve.

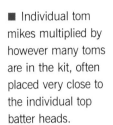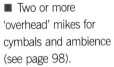

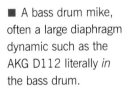

■ Individual tom mikes multiplied by however many toms are in the kit, often placed very close to the individual top batter heads.

■ Two or more 'overhead' mikes for cymbals and ambience (see page 98).

■ A hi-hat mike, often close to the top cymbal.

■ Additional room ambience mikes, especially if the kit is being recorded in a special 'live' acoustic drum room. These are placed at a distance from the kit, sometimes even attached to the walls or ceiling as 'barrier effect' mikes.

For the engineer, so many microphones produces a plethora of phase and acoustic spill problems, often solved by the use of gates and EQ filters. Without a lot of time and care this can often result in a rather artificial 'processed' sound.

Despite this challenge, this approach has become ubiquitous and leads to a very different perception of drum sound, and presents many challenges for the drummer in the studio.

The bass drum king

The D112 has earned a well-deserved reputation as the best kick-drum microphone ever made. It needs to handle up to 160dB SPL without audible distortion.

The D12 series has always had a specially engineered diaphragm with a very low resonance frequency. This maintains a solid and powerful response below 100Hz. An additional narrow band presence rise at 4kHz ensures the mike punches through dense mixes with little or no added EQ.

Snare and toms

'Close miking' a drum is analogous to putting your ear an inch or two from the drum head – not something we do in the real world. What you hear in this microphone position is a 'sample' of the drum sound, usually part of the batter head sound and often omitting the sound of the resonant head and the shell resonance. The sound has lots of transient from the stick strike and often a surfeit of high harmonics (as you might expect). The chosen solution is often not moving the mike further from the drum – to give a broader sample – but sticking lots of gaffer tape or Moongel on the head to reduce the high harmonics. Not ideal.

Bass drum

Recording the bass drum, particularly in the analogue and vinyl era, was a struggle. Low frequencies were hard to get heard in the overall mix of a song, especially on then prevalent AM radio, and if your record didn't get AM radio play then it would flop. Consequently engineers and producers strived to give an audio illusion of a bass drum in the form of a 'click' at 1–4kHz; these are in the speech frequency band where the ear is at its most sensitive. Hence the tendency to place the bass drum mike in the drum and close to the inside of the batter head, where these high frequencies are most prevalent. The consequent 'click' was then compressed or limited so that 10dB in produced 1dB out! Frustrating.

In this era, resonance – especially in the difficult to mix low-frequency areas – was discouraged by the application of blankets, pillows, eiderdowns and stage weights! Witness Steve Gadd's solution in the case study of his Yamaha kit later in this book. Steve has spent a lot of his life in the studio, and to this day his bass drum has a folded-up removal van blanket in it.

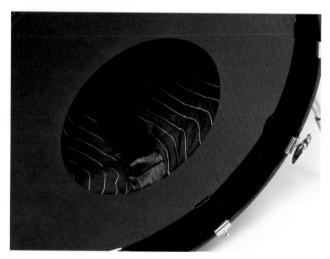

If all this wasn't enough, vinyl and AM radio encouraged an artificial and very limited dynamic range – only 4dB on most hit records. The singer was effectively 1dB louder than your whole kit and the band combined.

Digital glory?

I returned from Japan in 1988 with Britain's first Sony DAT recorder and thought the audio world stood on the brink of a dynamic revolution. I was wrong. But in the 21st century the digital era has well and truly arrived, bringing theoretical dynamic ranges of 90dB (almost the limit of what we can cope with) and 10Hz–20Khz of frequency spectrum (every frequency we're able to hear).

You would think recording techniques could change. And they have – a little. The snag is that old 'compressed and limited' axioms still apply. The music industry has become hooked on the notion of who's loudest wins. If your record sounds louder on MTV then more people will buy it! The easy route to loud is compression, and for drums 'click'.

Not everyone now subscribes to this approach, and the growth of unplugged acoustic sets and world percussion has encouraged engineers and producers to broaden their view of what can and is recorded, so we travel in hope.

Practical approaches

If you can make your kit sound great acoustically and the room acoustic is good, then encourage your engineer to try a simple three-microphone recording technique: a great matched stereo pair for the overall sound and a bass drum mike to lift the bass drum in the mix.

I've found through thousands of recording sessions that often the best place for the pair of stereo mikes is 'spaced' *behind* the drummer – giving his perspective on the kit, the one he plays to, tensions his drums to and gauges his dynamics from. This is not the same as 'overhead' miking, as that position often hears too much cymbal.

It's important to place the kit away from a sound-reflective wall and to use high quality omnidirectional mikes if you have them.

If the kit sounds good in the room, high quality capacitor 'omnis' will also hear that. The bass drum mike can also be outside the drum and take in the overall resonance of the sound.

Sound logical? Give it a try – you may save your engineer hours of grief with EQ, compression and gating, and you can leave the gaffer tape in the cupboard. I've often used this approach with Dave Mattacks, one of world's greatest session players, and it works. His kit arrives at the studio; he tensions it to the acoustic; it sounds great, and you record *that* sound – Vulcan logic.

Paul's 'Behind Heads'. The AKG414s are placed behind the drums, not over the cymbals.

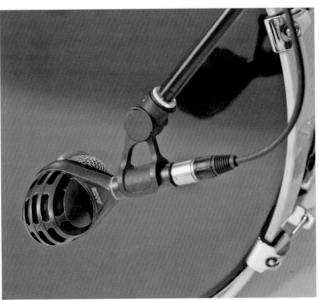

Some tips

Whatever microphone techniques your engineer employs, some things are universal:

- Good heads sound good – change your heads a week before recording and get them settled in.
- If it squeaks, oil it, pedals and hi-hats.
- If it rattles, damp it. A little foam rubber packing behind a noisy bolt works wonders.
- Use a simple stationery-type folder clip to keep a bass drum mike cable off the resonant head. Believe it or not a cable will inhibit the head; clip the cable to the hoop and you're free to boom!
- If some damping of excess high frequencies is required then try a little Moongel, discreetly applied. See page 41.

frequencies produced by the bass drum it can also be used in tandem with a standard microphone to deliver an extremely powerful wide-range sound. It also works effectively with a floor tom, bass guitar, low brass, etc. The mike has a standard XLR low-impedance output for mixing consoles.

Placement and proximity have an effect on the sound captured by the Subkick system, so experimentation with these variables will lead to a variety of tonal possibilities. Placing the Subkick in front of the head port, or at varied distances from the head itself, will produce a range of phase relationships with the drum sound.

Its three-legged stand has a ball clamp for easy adjustment of the microphone angle, and together with a tom clamp provides adequate stability, though a stage weight might be needed if there's any stage movement.

I imagine the Subkick might also be effective in a PA situation, though I've yet to try this.

ABOVE The Yamaha Subkick.

Feeling low?

For many years studio engineers have employed loudspeakers as microphones when low-frequency sounds elude even the large diaphragms of AKG D12s and similar. Russ Miller has packaged this idea into a tidy reality in the Yamaha Subkick, a very large-diameter microphonic diaphragm that captures bass drum sub-frequencies.

The Subkick consists of a 10in x 5in birch and Philippine mahogany seven-ply shell that houses a 16cm, 50W low-frequency driver cone. Whilst the large diameter enables the Subkick to capture the natural low

Practice pads and beyond

Like many drummers I've an ambivalent approach to practice pads. I know I need to keep my rudimental chops in, but the rubber pad can be so boring and the sound produced has nothing to do with my approach to music.

I'm always looking for something better. In the '60s I put together a tubular frame and a set of practice pads which enabled me to practise working around the kit without driving the neighbours crazy. However, the sounds were still exceptionally dull and uninspiring and the feel was all wrong.

■ The Limpet is quite a good idea. A thick rubber pad sits on the snare head and has two surfaces, hard at the centre and softer at the edge – this mutes the drum about 20dB but retains some snare response. This is good for quiet rudimental study.

■ The JEMM Practa Pal attaches to your knee for those moments when boredom sets in on the long road to a gig.

■ The Laptop from Rhythm Tech doesn't need batteries and is actually loud enough for an unplugged rehearsal in the hotel room, and has a real snare beneath the pad.

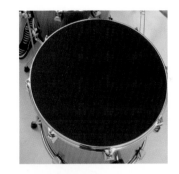

■ The Softapads from JHS offer the opportunity to play your familiar kit layout without causing a family disturbance. These simple foam pads come in a range of sizes and include an attachment for the bass drum.

■ The illustrated rubber pads from DrumTech extend the Limpet idea and include pads for cymbals.

■ For group teaching I found the Yamaha electronic pads really helpful – the sounds (on headphones) are very good, and the supplied backing tracks provide plenty of scope for experimenting. You can also record your efforts and listen back.

Protection racket – cases and gig bags

Though I've gigged the Premier kit case studied on page 124 since the mid-1960s, it's still looking good. When I bought the kit I took the then radical decision to buy fibre cases for all the drums. Though the cases were second-hand they've taken all the flak thrown at them, and apart from the hardware/snare case (after a few thousand gigs the locking clasps are giving up) they're holding up well.

BELOW Kinsman soft padded bags.

RIGHT Rigid ABS cases are very effective and lightweight.

So this was a great investment, and one I recommend. If, however, fibre or ABS cases are too bulky then the soft type from Kinsman and others will at least prevent scratches and damaged heads.

Protection Racket offer a great range of soft, semi-rigid and rigid cases. These cover all the usual drum sizes and also include a very substantial wheeled cymbal case, with soft lambswool inserts for the individual cymbals. They also do stick bags and drummers' tool cases.

ABOVE Protection Racket matched sets.

Bags for the tricky and easily damaged electronic kits have versatile dividers for keeping all the individual components protected.

Plastic sheaths for stands are also a neat idea that prevents a lot of scratched chromium.

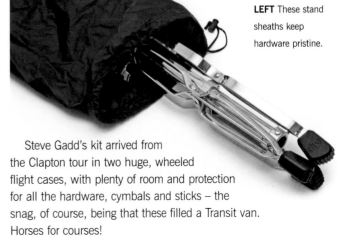

LEFT These stand sheaths keep hardware pristine.

Steve Gadd's kit arrived from the Clapton tour in two huge, wheeled flight cases, with plenty of room and protection for all the hardware, cymbals and sticks – the snag, of course, being that these filled a Transit van. Horses for courses!

Rewrapping a vintage drum

This mid-'60s drum has suffered severe cosmetic degradation
over the years and is also an 'odd' drum, in that I have no kit to
match it to. I do have a red glitter Premier kit, however (see page
124), and this is missing a 12in x 8in tom, so I'm going to try and
match this finish and give the 'odd' drum a new lease of life.

This drum is a pre-international size 12in – the
actual size, bearing edge to bearing edge, is more
like 11.5in – so the heads have to be ordered from
Remo, who do clear and coated Ambassadors for
these eccentric sizes.

Legendary London-based drum-maker and
restorer Eddie Ryan ordered some red sparkle
wrap from Italy via the USA (see *Useful contacts*
appendix). This glass glitter is a good match for the
original 1960s finish on the other 14in x 8in tom.

1 First remove the heads from the drum. Take the strain evenly from the hoop as usual, by cross de-tensioning. In the absence of a vintage slotted key I'm using a straight-slot screwdriver.

2 Remove the lugs from the drum with a No2 Phillips. A handy Tupperware container keeps all the bits together.

3 The vintage tom fitting bracket required a 5/16in wrench.

4 At some point a well-meaning previous owner has forced a standard-sized head on to the batter side of this drum, distorting the hoop in the process – witness the gap when laid on a flat surface. This was an added challenge, solved by Eddie's fortunate hoarding of an original amongst his collection of vintage parts. Straightening a bent die-cast hoop is almost impossible.

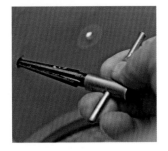

5 The vintage badge is removed by grinding the back off the retaining rivet with a rose countersink and then enlarging the hole slightly with a reaming tool.

6 Note the old wrap is fitted clear of the bearing edge.

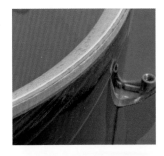

7 Eddie removed the old wrap by first scoring a line through it with a Stanley blade and then gently lifting with a decorators' scraper.

8 The shell is sanded lightly, both to remove the old glue and provide a key for the new adhesive.

9 The new wrap is cut to size on a large guillotine.

10 Eddie marks up the shell with a guideline and signs his work!

11 The bearing edge is going to need a little work.

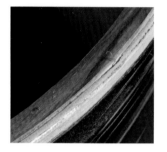

12 Eddie checked the bearing edge for gaps and inconsistencies with a piece of paper and the drum placed on a very flat terrazzo tile – the paper should not fit through the gap.

13 He then corrected the errors by gently sanding the bearing edge on another tile, which has self-adhesive abrasive paper glued to the very flat surface.

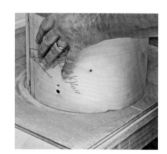

14 Eddie uses pegs to 'dummy run' the wrap in place and establish the best position for the wrap. Most repairers overlap the wrap about an inch these days, to avoid shrinkage exposing the shell. The overlap is usually disguised by positioning near some rear lugs.

15 Eddie's gluing method is his 'trade secret' – somehow he achieves good adherence without bubbles in the wrap. I suspect he may use carpet fitters' spray adhesive, but he's not telling, so I had to vacate the workshop for 20 minutes. Some repairers use a 'rolling' technique on a hard surface to remove any bubbles. Others use a decorators' roller, but as I've said, Eddie's secret method results in no bubbling. The rest of us just have to experiment.

16 Once the glue is set Eddie removed the protective film from the new wrap.

17 The wrap itself needed the edges removing initially with a Stanley knife, and then a series of grits – a medium Sandisk, then a P80 and then a 120.

21 A nice touch is added by Eddie's offer of a vintage 1960s Premier interior damper, the original having been lost from this drum. The replacement is bolted in place.

18 Because the glass glitter is prone to shatter Eddie starts the new lug-holes with a bradawl and then tidies these with a hand rose from the exterior rather than a drill from the interior.

22 Before refitting the heads Eddie lubricates each bolt with a little Vaseline. Note the important but easily forgotten washers. Eddie slightly over-tensions the head for seating and stretch.

19 A light buff with some polishing compound and the refitting of the lugs and vintage bracket almost completes the job.

23 He then tensions the head down to a lower pitch.

24 The drum sounds and looks good.

20 The Premier badge has to be glued in place, as the grommets are no longer available.

Drummer? Musician? Percussionist?

In purely practical terms most bands have one drummer, but many pro touring bands also employ a percussionist. Being versatile presents TWO employment prospects.

I strongly recommend any drummer with pro ambitions to learn a few basic grooves on *djembe*, congas and timbales and to get themselves a set of 'toys'.

My own kit drumming started to improve as I started thinking more about 'colour' and moving away from accents on 2 and 4 and trying a percussionist's 'lean' on 1 and 3.

History

Early kit players used a vast range of colour with their drum sets – the 'contraption' or 'traps' kits of the 1920s bristled with effects, 'temple blocks', woodblocks, cowbells, triangles and rattles. Gene Krupa played all this stuff in his early days, but with the arrival of his 1936 Radio King focussed a lot more on establishing the now classic four-drum kit. It was The Beatles who reintroduced percussion colour to pop music as they discovered the delights of Abbey Road Studio's 'toy' cupboard. If you listen closely you soon realise many classic Beatle tracks benefit from this imaginative variety. All the Tamla Motown hits feature brilliant use of tambourine, and many also use claves and guiro.

What you need

■ A trap tray gives you a handy place to stow all this stuff, within easy reach when needed. This one is from Rhythm Tech and fits any regular drum stand.

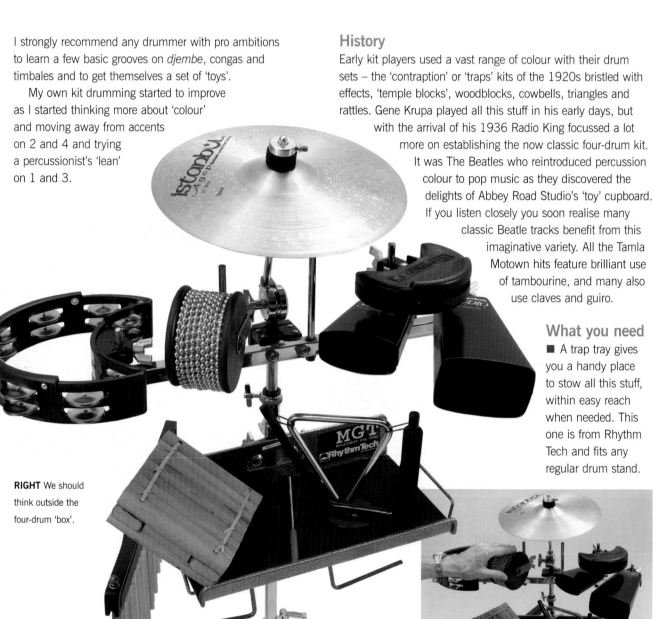

RIGHT We should think outside the four-drum 'box'.

■ Gibraltar also offer a versatile range of ratchet arms for suspending percussion.

■ Consider a percussion block for an alternative colour to the regular snare on the off beat.

■ Shakers are great for an intro groove. These dried 'beans' I hand-picked in the Caribbean, but a simple eggs and cocktail shaker can be more versatile.

■ Wind chimes played with a trailing finger are perfect for indicating a transition to a ballad chorus.

■ A splash cymbal is light enough to be played by hand, especially when the 'toys' are miked up.

■ Try a cowbell on the on beat. Two cowbells are even better, played African 'gong-gong' style as a flam.

■ A kit-mounted cabassa leaves your other hand free for cymbals and hi-hat.

■ *Djembe* and congas. I took a few *djembe* lessons in Africa, and most of the essential techniques cross over to congas. It's worth taking a short course to learn how to play 'off' the drums and to understand how congas complement the standard grooves. The trick is to work 'in' with the regular drummer and embellish and emphasise the beats he isn't! You'll need some J45 cream to keep your hands from splitting – if you think this is girly, tell that to the Mandinka drummers of the Gambia.

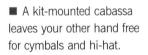

■ Jazz drummer Connie Kay taught me that hi-hat figures can be just as effective on a triangle, and lift a tune by the surprise of unexpected colour. This handy suspension won't 'turn' when in use.

■ A suspended tambourine makes for a contrasting colour in an intro off beat.

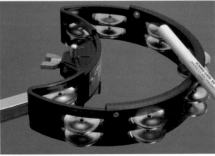

■ Timbales are great as a sparing effect. Like a set of metallic toms they cut through everything and can really give a mundane chorus a lift. Timbale sticks usually have no 'beads', but you can use conventional sticks just as effectively. Duran Duran used timbales to great effect on some early hits and left me with a studio full of splintered drumsticks. Santana's Karl Perazzo and Alex Acuna are your guides.

There are literally thousands of percussion possibilities from every corner of the world and I recommend you try them all. Mickey Hart's *Planet Drum* and *Drumming at The Edge of Magic* book and CD projects offer some great insight and many inspiring and practical ideas.

DRUM-KIT MANUAL

Specific case studies

These case studies range across the practical history of the modern drum kit. With the Slingerland Radio King kit as a beginning, we progress through Premier and Ludwig four-drum 1960s kits, through the Japanese-dominated '80s and to the early 21st-century four-tom double-pedal concert kit. Hardware has improved dramatically during this period, with a much greater stability and reliability than was dreamt of in the 1930s. However, drum tech Eddie Ryan and many other experts feel that the drums themselves are not necessarily better. Wood scarcities and mass production have perhaps played a part in less attention being paid to manufacturing detail. Perhaps drums improve with age. Certainly Charlie Watts will never part with his vintage Gretsch, and my '60s Premier has a distinct sound.

LEFT A snare for every backbeat.

Gene Krupa-style Slingerland 'Radio King' kit

Finished in classic white marine pearl, this type of kit was first manufactured in 1936 as 'The Radio King' for drum pioneer Gene Krupa. With its now classic layout this set marks the beginning of the modern drum kit.

Gene Krupa (1909–1973)

Gene Krupa's modern drum style, his insistence on being able to tune both heads on his toms, and his adoption of the ride cymbal, mark him out as the founder of the modern drum kit. From 1936 he played a Slingerland kit not unlike our case study, and his flamboyance meant he was noticed – drummers had arrived! If you want to see him in action check out *The Benny Goodman Story* biopic, especially *Sing Sing Sing* and hear a simple paradiddle turn into a sparkling solo. It's fascinating how after the excesses of the 1980s many drummers are now returning to a kit not so different from that played by Krupa – all you need for a solid groove.

Condition on arrival

This kit is in fine working order, having been lovingly cleaned and polished by current owner drummer Dave Brown of Wigan, England. Dave acquired the kit in London in 1998. The 'Krupa' model snare is from the 1930s and the rest of the kit probably from the 1940s or early '50s, though exact dating is very difficult. I had the kit for just 3 hours!

General description

The kit comprises a typical Krupa 1936 'Radio King' drum arrangement: one mounted tom and one floor-mounted tom, though Krupa often used two floor-mounted toms – a 16in x 16in and a 16in x 18in – all finished in this white marine pearl laminate. The sticks included for scale are period rosewood.

Made in the 1930s–1950s by the Slingerland Banjo and Drum Co, Corner Belden Avenue and Ward Street, Chicago, Illinois, USA

The snares

The kit has two associated snares, a WMP and a Gene Krupa. The 14in x 6.5in snare has a Fiberskyn 3 textured batter in place of the original calf head, and a clear modern snare head with eight tension rods per head in a combined lug.

■ The outer shell has the Slingerland badge on the shell and 'Radio King' engraving on the hoop. The 10mm vent hole is integral to the badge.

■ Note the adjustable green felt internal damper.

■ The tuning bolts specifically require a modern square drum key for tuning.

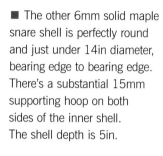

■ The other 6mm solid maple snare shell is perfectly round and just under 14in diameter, bearing edge to bearing edge. There's a substantial 15mm supporting hoop on both sides of the inner shell. The shell depth is 5in.

■ The batter head side of the shell has an interesting bearing edge with a rounded peak to the 35° angle on the inner edge.

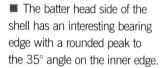

■ The rims are double-flanged metal 'stick choppers' with square tension bolts. The vintage Leedy sticks overpage have lead counterweights built into the butt ends. Heavy metal.

■ The snare mechanism is an adjustable throw-off. The snares are secured with string looped through the 16-strand single-course steel wire snares.

■ The lugs all have washers secured with a 6mm straight-slot.

■ The Krupa snare would originally have had an internal heater to keep the ascorbic calf heads dry and at tension. The mounting holes have been discreetly disguised.

■ Both snares sounds damn good – less like a whip crack and more like a drum!

Hardware

■ **Snare stand**
The lightweight single-braced stand is a 'Marvel' by Slingerland.

■ **Cymbal stands**
These flimsy stands were OK for the small, light cymbals of the 1930s, but when Gene became famous enough to have a road crew he used custom-made stands adapted from music stands, with heavy cast bases. He needed these, as he became the first drummer to use a 24in ride cymbal. Krupa always used Avedis Zildjian cymbals, and this is one of my own Istanbul-made Ks.

■ **Hi-hat**
The lightweight Slingerland hi-hat is substantial for the era, and the cymbals are the large bell type from the 1920s and '30s.

■ **Bass-drum pedal**
This is very advanced for an early pedal and has double springs.

Bass drum
A large 24in x 14in,
though Gene preferred
an even larger 26in shell!

■ The drum has wooden
hoops and modern Slingerland-
branded Remo heads.

■ There are ten individual lugs
per head. The hoops and heads
are tensioned with substantial
metal claws. These have stylish
timpani-style handles.

■ The three-ply shell is a
typical Radio King mahogany/
poplar/mahogany, and there
are many discrete repairs to
the drum following 80 years
of adapted use.

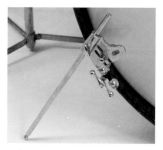

■ The resonant head has two dampers,
a 'modern' 1960s-style internal felt strip and a
1930s external damping pad. The hidden badge
is 'BR', as Buddy Rich also used this brand of
kit at the beginning and end of his career.

■ There are rim mounts for
a cowbell, but sadly the Slingerland
cowbell has been lost in action. Krupa
often had a splash cymbal and bell
also attached to the back rim. His
smaller cymbals were shell-mounted,
though he used the unreliable rim
mounts as shown for some years.

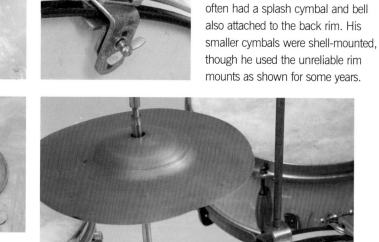

■ The drum has two
Slingerland rim-mounted
spurs. These were
common until the mid-
'60s and always fell off at
a critical moment! 'Bass
drum roll' often took on
a whole new meaning.

Tom 2

16in x 16in, weight unknown. Constructed exactly as tom 1, with eight lugs per head and the same head configuration and bearing edge. It is floor-mounted, with elementary wing-nut height adjustment.

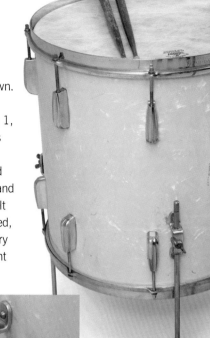

Tom 1

9in x 13in, weight unknown. Note that the suspended tom is rim-mounted. This was poor engineering, and you knew about it when the tom landed on your foot!

All the tom hoops are the double-flanged chromed type as on the snare, with six lugs per head on this drum. The lugs are substantial and marked a departure from the earlier tube lugs.

■ The shell is 6mm thick, perfectly round, and the interior clear-lacquered. Note the round double-headed adjustable damper.

■ The resonant and batter bearing edges are 35°, all slightly rounded off.

■ The heads are Remo Fiberskyn 3.

Signed off

This remarkable kit changed drumming forever. Gene daringly eschewed the 1920s contraption kit and made drums and drumming sexy.

'The beat, beat, beat of the tom-tom when the Jungle shadows fall...Night and Day!'

NB Try not to trip on the flimsy single braces as you take a bow.

Classic Ludwig 'Downbeat' kit

27 years on from Krupa's Radio King little had changed in the drum department. The bigger cymbals and mylar headswere both about volume and being heard – but 'the groove machine' remains essentially the same.

Ringo Starr and Ludwig

Ringo played Ajax and Premier kits before switching to Ludwig after the first Beatles album. He was initially attracted to the Black Oyster Pearl finish but must have loved the sound of those mahogany/poplar/mahogany toms – I know I did. He first played the Downbeat kit at Birmingham's ATV studios on 12 May 1963 for the Lew Grade TV show *Thank Your Lucky Stars*. The kit was a special order from Ivor Arbiter's Drum City, Shaftesbury Avenue, London WC2.

Getting up and running

Yard Gavrilovic of Vintage DrumYard has set this kit up pretty much as Ringo likes his – those are even Ringo's sticks. The big difference is no Rogers Swiv-O-Matic tom mount; more on that later. The snare is a metal 'Supraphonic 400' of the type Ringo used later, though he initially preferred a wooden 'Jazz Festival' snare in matching Oyster Pearl.

General description

The kit comprises the small sizes Ringo requested for his first kit: a 20in x 14in bass drum, one mounted 12in x 8in tom and one 14in x 14in floor-mounted tom. He would later add larger sizes as he tried to compete with the screams of Beatlemania in an era when drums were not miked to the PA.

Made in 1964 and assembled in Chicago, USA. Total weight 33kg

The snare

14in x 5in, 3.91kg. This lightweight Ludwig 'Supraphonic 400' is most likely made of 'Ludalloy', though there are some 1960s chrome on brass snares. The drum has a Remo USA coated Ambassador batter and a thin clear 'Weatherking' snare head with ten individual tension rods per head.

■ The chromed shell has the 'no serial number' type of Keystone badge.

■ The snare mechanism is a simple throw-off and the snares are tensioned with string looped through the 17-strand single-course steel wire snares. Fine adjustment is via a recessed thumbscrew.

■ The hoops are triple-flanged pressed metal with standard square tension bolts.

■ The shell is perfectly round and approx 13.75in diameter, bearing edge to bearing edge.

■ The tuning bolts require a 0.2in square drum key for tuning and the bolt thread is a standard modern 3/16in–24G.

■ The snare has an adjustable internal damper which has the baseball-bat type tone control usually associated with Ludalloy shells.

■ This snare sounds really bright, with a cutting crack for the backbeat. The only snag is the chrome tends to fall off!

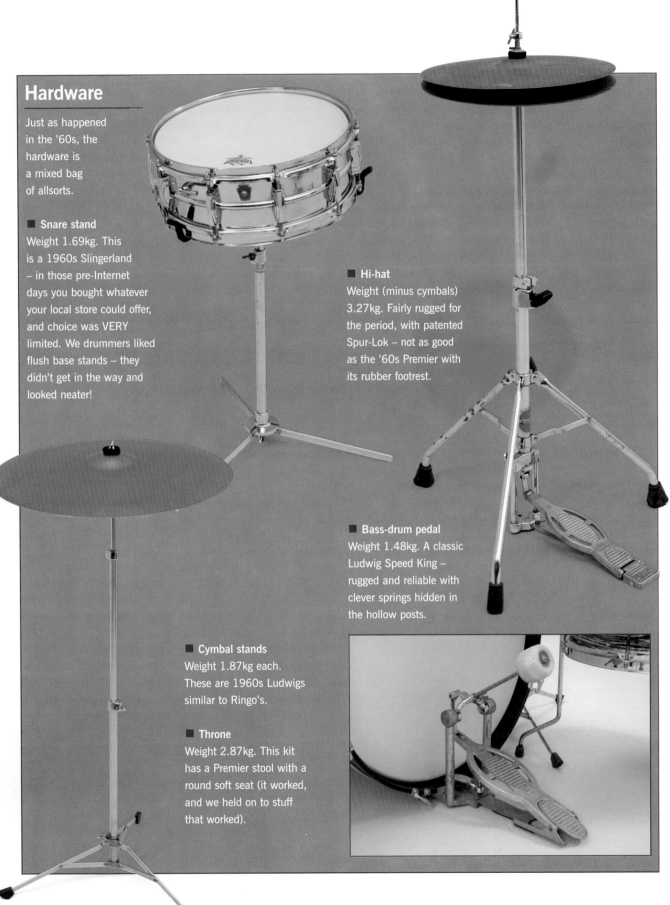

Hardware

Just as happened in the '60s, the hardware is a mixed bag of allsorts.

■ **Snare stand**
Weight 1.69kg. This is a 1960s Slingerland – in those pre-Internet days you bought whatever your local store could offer, and choice was VERY limited. We drummers liked flush base stands – they didn't get in the way and looked neater!

■ **Hi-hat**
Weight (minus cymbals) 3.27kg. Fairly rugged for the period, with patented Spur-Lok – not as good as the '60s Premier with its rubber footrest.

■ **Bass-drum pedal**
Weight 1.48kg. A classic Ludwig Speed King – rugged and reliable with clever springs hidden in the hollow posts.

■ **Cymbal stands**
Weight 1.87kg each. These are 1960s Ludwigs similar to Ringo's.

■ **Throne**
Weight 2.87kg. This kit has a Premier stool with a round soft seat (it worked, and we held on to stuff that worked).

- The heads are Ludwig-branded 'WeatherMasters'.

- There are eight individual lugs and claws per head, all with timpani handles.

- The bass drum has two fold-out legs. These revolve through 90° and tighten with a wing nut. These were an improvement on the rim-mounted types but still rather insubstantial for rock'n'roll.

Bass drum

A small 20in x 14in, weight 7.57kg. Ringo later switched to a 22in bass drum but this was the size associated with the first American tour.

- The bass drum's wooden hoop is secured with a Ludwig drum anchor. These were the best of the bunch but still largely ineffective. This particular drum is in good shape – unfortunately many Ludwig kits of this era were rushed out of the factory to meet a surge of 'Beatlemania' demand, and many were not quite round!

- Note the Ludwig 'rail-consolette' tom bar – this was versatile but tended to slip, as well as needing a specific spanner, which encouraged Ringo to quickly switch to the Rogers Swiv-O-Matic, which is the basis of many modern ball-joint fittings.

- The famous 'drop T' Beatles logo was executed by Eddie Stokes, a jobbing signwriter working for Arbiters. Ivor Arbiter charged £5 for designing and Eddie's painting of perhaps the most famous graphic logo in music history. Seven or eight versions of the drumhead were made over the next few years.

Tom 1

12in x 8in, weight 2.9kg. Again this is Ringo's original size, but he later (circa 1966) moved up to 13in x 9in. The sticks included for scale are Ringo's own signature Pro Marks and date from his 2008 tour.

All the tom hoops are the triple-flanged chromed type, with six substantial lugs per head.

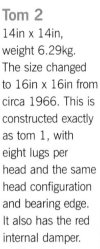

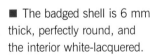

■ The badged shell is 6 mm thick, perfectly round, and the interior white-lacquered.

■ Note the early '60s red damper – these switched to white for the late '60s.

■ The resonant and batter bearing edges are 45° on the inside – all slightly rounded off.

■ The heads are a coated Ambassador batter and a clear Ambassador resonant.

Tom 2

14in x 14in, weight 6.29kg. The size changed to 16in x 16in from circa 1966. This is constructed exactly as tom 1, with eight lugs per head and the same head configuration and bearing edge. It also has the red internal damper.

The tom legs are fairly substantial splayed types, adjusted with a hardware-store wing nut.

Signed off

The current Ludwig reissue version of this kit offers maple/poplar/maple but Yard tells me this one uses mahogany/poplar/mahogany – and it sounds like mahogany.

This is the kit – simply miked, with an overhead and a bass drum mike – that launched more hits than anything before or since. Forget all that clever stuff, give the song a winning groove. Thanks, Ringo.

1960s vintage Premier kit

These Premier kits were the mainstay of British Rock 'n Roll from the late '50s to the mid-'60s. American kits were then difficult to obtain and cost twice as much!

Getting up and running

The drums still work well and have very minimal signs of age. New heads are all that's required for a good 'vintage' sound.

General description

My kit comprises the classic 1960s four drums: one mounted tom, a floor tom, a metal 'Royal Ace' snare and a bass drum. The shells are three-ply birch, finished here in Red Glitter but also then available in Gold Glitter, Aquamarine, Silver and Duraplastic Mahogany, Pearl, Blue, Burgundy, Marine and Solid Black. We also have two cymbal stands, a hi-hat and bass-drum pedal and a small 12in x 8in tom from the Premier museum.

Condition on arrival

This is the author's own kit, purchased in Liverpool in the mid-'60s. The drums were bought in instalments, as the approximate kit cost of £150 was beyond the reach of a gigging teenager. Consequently the art deco/nouveau lugs vary slightly, reflecting the 1964–66 design variants.

Over the ensuing 40-plus years, several items have been stolen, so the bass-drum pedal, stands and cowbell have been kindly borrowed from the Leicester Premier Museum to give a sense of this kit's original state. All the drums have their original Premier fibre cases. I also have two pairs of late '60s 'E' sticks in hickory and one pair of 'Cs' in lancewood. Lancewood sticks were rather heavy and also soft, so we always erred towards the expensive imported American hickory. Eventually Premier came up with their own hickory sticks.

Originally all the heads were Premier's own 'Everplay Extras'. These are still intact on the (Premier museum) 12in x 8in tom, my bass drum resonant head and the Royal Ace snare head. This Premier kit has great historical significance, as apart from minor cosmetic changes and a 3in wooden snare it's the type used for the first year of Beatles recordings from 6 June 1962 to 12 May 1963, by both Pete Best and Ringo Starr. This takes in (most takes of) the first three Beatles singles and the first album, *Please Please Me*.

Interestingly when asked to change his kit by Brian Epstein, Ringo chose a Trixon, but was drawn to a colour swatch of the famous Black Oyster Pearl and was told he could only have *that* finish in Ludwig. According to Ivor Arbiter, Ringo apparently didn't ask about the sound or whether it was birch or maple – that's the way it was in 1963, we were just grateful to have four decent drums.

Ringo's Premier kit – seen in the Abbey Road pictures of Harry Hammond and traded in part-exchange for the Ludwig – was finished in mahogany Duraplastic.

From the Premier Drum Company of Leicester, England, circa 1964–66.

The snare

14in x 5.5in Royal Ace, weight 4.2kg. Introduced in 1960, the all-metal Royal Ace has Premier's patented parallel floating snare mechanism that maintains the snares at tension even when released. There are two parallel sets of ten strands.

■ The rims are solid cast Mazac alloy as also used by Gretsch, chrome plated. All the tension rods have a vintage 'coin' slot adjustment – handy when your drum key goes AWOL. British pennies naturally give a better tone. Each bolt has a steel washer; nylon was a rare and expensive luxury in 1965. The bolt thread is a standard modern 3/16in–24G.

■ The eight full-width lugs are all still working, though the chrome has just started to pit in the sweaty areas around the snare release. There is no cushion material between the lugs and shell and the threads have no modern internal 'anti-rattle' soft plastic damper, but the lugs are very accurately engineered. These lugs are the 1958-pattern 'rounded Art Nouveau'. Art nouveau and deco design elements go back as far as Premier's time at London's Park Royal, when they had a factory close to design icons such as the famous Hoover Building and Park Royal station.

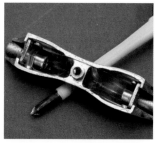

It has a single-ply Remo 'Weather King' Ambassador textured batter and a thin clear Everplay Extra snare head with eight individual tension rods per head. The heavy 'Diamond' outer chrome shell is suitably badged with the pre-'66 Premier logo. I have since changed the heads to Evans coated batter and a Hazy snare.

The Premier story

Established in 1922 by Fred and Albert Della Porta and George Smith at 47 Berwick Street in London's Soho, the Premier Drum Company subsequently moved to nearby Golden Square (now Footes' premises) and eventually Park Royal in Acton. However, the Blitz of 1940 forced Premier out to Leicester, where they still have offices and a fascinating collection of vintage kits. In 1966 – the period of some of our vintage kit – they won the Queen's Award to Industry.

■ The chromed shell is perfectly round and 13.75in diameter, bearing edge to bearing edge.

■ The batter head bearing edge has a sharp angle of 62°, contributing to the drum's very bright sound. The snare head bearing edge is the same, with the parallel snare arrangement obviating any need for a snare-bed indentation.

What to look for in a vintage Premier

Many vintage Premier 1960s kits have survived due to their sturdy construction and heavily chromed die-cast parts. Look for:

■ Straight hoops – unfortunately many vintage hoops are distorted due to uneven tensioning and people trying to fit international-size heads.

■ Intact bearing edges, especially the lower head. These are often pitted by damage inflicted during the 1970s trend for single-headed drums.

■ Be aware of the vintage slotted tension bolts – you'll need a vintage key or a coin of the realm.

■ The snare mechanism is a complex but beautifully engineered parallel release, and the snares are tensioned the full width of the head but floating from the shell. The snare tension is adjusted via two thumbwheels, one each side of the head.

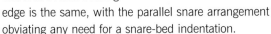

■ The batter head has a '60s era internal adjustable felt damper. These were very common in the '50s and '60s but not really that useful – they killed the higher order harmonics but left the drum sounding dull.

■ The inner shell thickness is only .75mm including the chrome plating. This contributes to the sound of the drum, and as a bonus minor dents can be literally pushed out with your thumb – be careful, however, as if you overdo this you could easily distort the whole shell!

■ The vent hole is an open 5mm, cleverly disguised in the P of the logo.

Hardware

I was never able to afford the then state of the art Premier flush stands, so the two stands and snare stand are borrowed from Premier. I have an old Olympic snare stand (Olympic were Premier's 'Squier' brand in this period) and a Gigster cymbal stand left over from my first kit; Ringo had the same mishmash – we bought whatever we could afford, usually second-hand. The hi-hat is original and I bought it for its lower cymbal-tilt mechanism, which was innovative at the time. I also had the matching art deco 250 pedal but this and the drum stool with its original excruciatingly hard rubber bicycle seat were stolen at the BBC in the 1980s.

■ **250 bass drum pedal**
Weight 1.25kg. As supplied the 250 had a dual-sided beater, soft lambswool one side and leather on cork the other, though in an attempt to be heard in the days before drum kits were ever miked up I followed the example of Bobby Elliot from The Hollies and used a solid felt beater; then as guitar amps changed to Marshall 'stacks' a solid wooden beater.

Many pedals of the time still had leather linkages, which tended to break, and the all-metal approach of the 250 was a welcome step forward. The bottom rivet tended to fail after a few years as here, but

it's been DIY-replaced with a split rivet. The substantial rim clamp was also welcome, as many pedals of this era fell off the drum mid-gig – very embarrassing!

■ **Hi-hat**
Weight 3.75kg.

The flush-based stand was substantial for the era and sometimes stayed where it was put. There are no memory locks. The drive is direct via a sprung linkage.

The lower cymbal has a cushioned cup seating, with variable tilt preventing a 'silent' hi-hat.

The upper cymbal clutch is not original, though exactly the same in simple terms and traditionally cushioned with some felts.

The pedal has a fairly substantial (for the period) pressed steel platform and an art deco plastic overlay with double fixing spurs on the heel. The plastic overlay tended to come off and mine was re-glued twice.

This hi-hat has done hundreds of gigs without letting me down.

The adjustable tension single spring made for a fast return stroke as bass drum patterns started to become more intricate. The heel spikes were also innovative and welcome. I know how popular this pedal was because two of mine were stolen!

■ Two 1960s cymbal stands

Weight 1.8kg each.

These flush stands were much appreciated on the tiny stages of The Cavern and The Grave, where every inch of saved space counted, and such stands were reasonably stable as long as the stage didn't wobble! They have contrasting tilt mechanisms, the latter of which was a big improvement on the earlier type with washer and felt cymbal protectors, though the range of tilt is limited (see below).

There are no memory locks and the single levers tended to fail, causing a dramatic and unexpected crash. For some reason the older stand has a lower centre of gravity than the newer one.

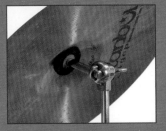

■ Snare stand

Weight 2kg. This compact flush-based stand has no memory locks and a tilt mechanism still dependent on hardware-store wing nuts. The 'basket' would originally have had rubber sleeving snare protectors, but these tended to perish and disintegrate and have disappeared here.

■ Cowbell

A 1950s trend towards Latin music meant every '60s drum kit came with a cowbell. This led to the fab intro on the Rolling Stones' *Honky Tonk Women*. These heavily chromed Premier items looked great but sounded a bit quaint. We sought out more earthy items!

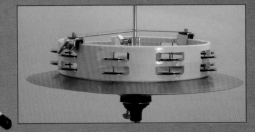

■ The 'ching ring'

This 1960s take on the tambourine hi-hat amalgam was sold without a hi-hat clutch but definitely worked better with one. This added colour to the off beat for many '60s classics.

■ Throne

These fold-up stools meant the whole kit could fit into four fibre cases. This was very critical in the days before road crews, when I sometimes carried my whole kit for a mile. This one from the Premier museum has the 'luxury' round cushion – heaven! Drum stools were a relatively rare luxury in the 1960s.

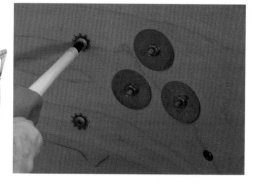

■ The vintage tom holder is secured to the shell by three bolts that go through into the shell cavity.

Bass drum
22in x 17in,
weight 7kg.

■ The bass drum's 11mm x 42mm wooden hoops have the Red Glitter inlaid into the surface.

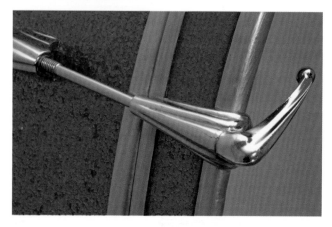

■ The hoops and heads are tensioned with some fairly substantial cast metal claws and utilise the vintage approach with thumb tension bolts. These fittings all do the job and are holding up well.

■ The puny Meccano-like tom bracket is secured with thumb locks. Keith Moon, who also favoured Premier Red Sparkle, quickly gave up on his Premier fittings and used Rogers Swiv-O-Matics, which were far sturdier.

■ The bass drum has two insubstantial retractable 8cm spurs that had optional and adjustable rubber feet or spikes. These were novel for the time and far better than the previous bolt-on spurs (which invariably fell off).

■ The 16 lugs are full width, which takes the strain of the shell. They're 1958 rounded art nouveau type as found on the snare and smallest tom.

■ The bass drum originally had 2in x 3in felt strips running down the centre of both heads for built-in damping – Ringo used these, but he offset the strip to one side. There were no two-ply heads or 'edge-muffled' heads available in the 1960s.

■ The drum was originally anchored with a small spiked bracket attached to the bottom front hoop. These didn't work, and some drummers would actually nail their front hoop to the stage! I used a 9in strip of 2in x 1in timber and a carpenters' gimlet as a 'door stop'. This practice was very unpopular with club secretaries, as the stage soon resembled an attack from a plague of termites. I countered by always using the same hole for reappearances at the same club. Stone and glass stages, however, presented a challenge...

■ The birch shell thickness is 4mm (substantially thinner than modern six-ply shells) including the plastic laminate, and this thin shell has to bear the weight of the mounted toms. The heads are given extra support by two 15mm beech hoops at the leading edge.

■ The bearing edge has a rounded, roughly 70° angle, the rounding intended to give a warmer bias to the tone.

Specific maintenance

■ All the lug bolts need cleaning and lubrication.
■ The snare could do with a good clean-out – it has 40 years of dust in the snare head. (See page 87.)
■ The snare strands could do with replacement, as one strand is distorted. ADC drums of Liverpool can supply replicas of these vintage types.

■ The snares are removed with a 2.5mm straight-slot screwdriver.
■ The nylon friction bushings on the snare mechanism could do with a little light lubrication – I'm using Planet Waves' Lubrikit.

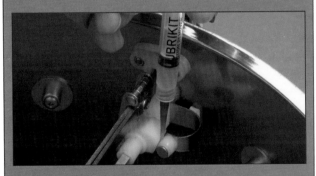

■ The small tom resonant bearing edge will need some attention – see page 86.
■ New heads for the whole kit would lift the sound and make a tuning easier – see page 82.
■ The broken thumbscrew thread on the tom fitting needs attention – it currently doesn't tighten. It will need a rethread at a larger size.
■ All the bass drum and tom lugs had worked loose – a No 2 Phillips does the job. I tightened all the other fittings at the same time, which required an 8mm socket spanner and a No 1 Phillips steadying the external screws.

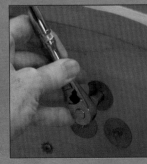

Tom 1

12in x 8in, weight 3.25kg. This comes from the Premier museum.

Note the suspended toms are shell-mounted not RIMS isolated as on most modern kits (shell mounting may inhibit the shell resonance – see page 90). These toms have a chrome barrel-type mount that was fairly inflexible and made the initial siting a bit of a nightmare.

The rims are the same cast type as the snare, with six full-width lugs per head. The lugs are 10.5cm long, larger than on the snare but the same shape, and the tuning bolts have a 'coin'-type slot.

■ The shell is 4.5mm thick, perfectly round and the interior unlacquered, with a rounded bearing edge angle of approximately 61°. Unfortunately the bearing edge suffered some damage in the '70s when exposed as a DIY 'concert tom'. This exposure has led to some rust on the internal lug washers.

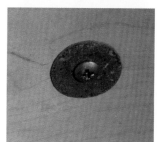

■ The internal adjustable damper is of the late-'50s type with two felt roundels rather than the later single pad.

Tom 2

14in x 8in, weight 4kg. This is constructed exactly as tom 1, but with eight lugs per head. The lugs have the flared art deco style of circa 1965. I custom-ordered this then unusual size tom from the Premier factory. It later became a favourite of The Who's Keith Moon, who preferred three 14in x 8in toms mounted over two bass drums.

The internal damper is the mid-'60s single-pad type.

Tom 3

16in x 20in,
weight 7kg.

■ This
floor tom
is a pre-
international
size and
needs pre-
international
heads,
currently only
available
from Remo
in a limited
range of types.
The current batter
is a pinstripe oil-filled
Remo, though
I'm about to change
this for a single-ply.

■ The unusual 20in
depth was originally
designed for British
drummer Eric Delaney,
a great showman of the
1940s and '50s.

■ This tom has three simple
spring-loaded clamps securing
the 10mm legs, which are
supposed to have rubber feet.
The adjustable legs have no
memory lock – these were
unheard of in the '60s .The three
rubber feet are missing in action;
these should be replaced, as
they'll affect the sound.

■ Note all the drum fittings
– lugs and brackets – were a
fraction loose due to 45 years of
playing. It's worth tightening all of
these before attuning the kit, as
inevitably something will rattle.

■ The rims and shells
follow the pattern of the
larger mounted tom, with
the same shell bearing edge
angle and the later-type
built-in damper.

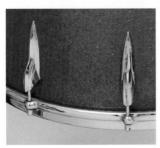

Signed off

I love this kit – it recalls so many gigs and so many funny
stories. It was even stolen once and turned up abandoned on
Liverpool's East Lancashire Road roundabout two days later
– still cased and undamaged. I'd put out a rumour in the
clubs that it was all custom-made and easily identifiable;
thankfully the thieves swallowed the myth.

The original cymbals are a 20in Zyn sizzle and 14in
super Zyn hi-hats, both of which are fairly poor. However,
I did splash out on a 20in Avedis Zildjian (£29 10s in 1966),
which is *still* good.

NB Late '60s
Premier drums often
have mahogany
shells, revealed by the
darker wood, lighter
weight and different
sound. Note the later
Premier badge and the
international-size ink
stamp inside the shell.

During the mid-1970s Premier used African mahogany
in their drum construction. Drums from that period were
mostly made of three-ply mahogany with beechwood
reinforcing hoops (or glue rings.). True mahogany from
Khaya Nyasica, Africa, provides an approximate 20%
increase in low-frequency resonance over maple drums.
Mid and high frequencies are mostly the same from a
reproduction point of view, but because the mahogany has
the 20% low-end increase the perceived tone is warmer.
However, the mahogany is a little frail.

Drum Workshop 'Jazz Series' kit

This kit epitomises the attention to detail, quality of material and excellent construction of DW products.

The Drum Workshop

Founded in 1972, Drum Workshop began as a teaching studio run by Don Lombardi. He originally offered private lessons and the occasional workshop. However, Lombardi, along with student (and current senior executive vice president) John Good, began a small drum equipment sales operation to cover their costs. After success with a height-adjustable throne and a good double bass drum pedal, DW took over established manufacturer Camco. These Camco origins can still be observed in DW's signature round 'turret' tuning lugs, designed by George H. Way and originally featured on 'George Way' drums.

DW expanded into larger facilities in Oxnard, California, and pioneered the timbre-matching technique of grouping a set of drum shells together by listening to the fundamental frequency of each shell before it's sanded. Each shell is stamped on the inside with the fundamental note of that shell. DW now offer both pre-made standard-sized sets as well as custom drums to customer specs. John Good told me: 'To understand a drum shell I had to really understand the veneer. Now, imagine I'm standing in front of you with a piece of veneer and it's maybe 3ft long 10in wide and 1/36in thick and the grain is running from left to right. That will sit on my hand so nice and strong it will barely flex from one side to another, and that's really the integrity of the strength of the grain direction. 'Now if I take that and have you tap on the top of the veneer and I bend it with both hands to make it bow like a saw blade – it will ascend a scale and pitch up. And there's a definite note value. All wood possesses a musical note value, some people don't realise that. When you put tension on that veneer the pitch goes up.'

Getting up and running

The drums are supplied fully assembled and about ten minutes should see it fully rigged, with the memory locks set for future gigs. The tuning is currently a suitably high 'jazz' pitch on the snare, with a surprisingly deep resonant response from the toms. The kit comes with a DW bag of useful bits including a DVD and spare lug bolts, drum keys and memory locks.

General description

This kit could be finished in any DW option but looks great in white twisted silk. Lacquers and satin bursts are all available. All options are hand-finished.

Assembled in the USA from
US and imported components

The snare

14in x 5.5in, weight 4.75kg. The snare has a DW-branded singly-ply Remo USA coated batter with numbered lug points, and a thin, milky clear Remo resonant head with a generous ten tension rods per head. The outer shell has the DW signature badge and serial number 12604.

■ The hoops are die-cast as standard on DW Jazz Shells. Their extra weight gives a drum more attack and less sustain. These drums are available with triple-flanged pressed hoops on request.

■ The lug thread inserts also have an internal nylon bushing to further prevent rattle and slippage. DW are very serious about a good rattle-free drum.

■ The tuning bolts require a 0.2in square drum key for tuning, and the bolt thread is an unusual 5mm 'True-Pitch' Tuning Rod, not the common 3/16in–24G. True-Pitch tuning rods are essentially tension rods with finer threads. The rods feature 5/32in–32G threads. This gives one thread every .08mm (about 20% more threads), versus one thread every 1.05mm on most other drums. The result is potentially easier, more precise pitching.

■ The 20 full-width lugs are very substantial and the snare is the only drum in the kit without individual lugs for each head. Each bolt has two washers, one chromed steel and one synthetic. These disparate materials naturally bind, helping prevent pitch slippage. Cleverly the chrome washer is undersize for the thread and remains on the bolt when de-tensioned.

■ The seven-ply shell is perfectly round and 13 7/8in diameter, bearing edge to bearing edge. The timbre note is F and the serial number is 795216. Signed by John and Don.

■ The single 7mm vent hole is lined with a chrome nut and bolt (which can come loose, causing an annoying rattle, so check this is secured internally, which requires a 14mm socket wrench).

■ The inner shell is unobstructed and beautifully gloss-lacquered and the shell thickness is a thin 8.8mm, including the wrap. Note the conventional straight seams in the ply.

■ The batter-head side of the shell has a DW 'butter edge' bearing edge with a rounded 60° angle on the inside edge and a soft curve on the outer edge, all contributing to the sound of the drum.

■ The snare-head bearing edge is the same. However, there's a very subtle, almost imperceptible snare-bed indentation at both snare junctions, only visible against a straight edge.

■ The snares are coarse-tensioned with a standard drum key and strip of clear plastic. This is looped through the 49mm wide 20-strand single-course stainless steel wires. The snares have brass end plates and fine adjustment is via an easily accessible thumbscrew; this also has a neat throw-off for 'no snare' sounds.

■ This snare sounds crisp and penetrating but with no annoying dissonance in the overtones.

■ All DW snares come with 'True-Tone' snare wires and, since 2009, the DW 'Mag Throw-off'. This snare throw-off system uses a three-way butt plate with three different settings – loose, medium and tight tension. This uses magnets to keep the snare throw-off in the 'on' position, and makes subtly changing the sound of the snare mid-gig much easier. In practice the quick switch from a 'wet' buzzy snare sound to a 'dry' tight sound is really useful.

Professional detail

DW make kits for every genre of popular music and this kit demonstrates the high quality and attention to detail that have given this US company their current status.

This specific kit is squarely aimed at the jazz combo and session market where a small finely honed kit is guaranteed to produce a musical and easily recorded ensemble. This set would also be perfect for laying down a killer groove for most pop and film sessions, an area traditionally dominated by the smaller Gretsch 'Jazz' kits.

The kit comprises a classic four-drum arrangement – one mounted tom, one floor tom, a snare and bass drum. All the hardware is an optional extra – here I have three cymbal stands, a hi-hat, and a single DW 9000 bass-drum pedal.

All the drums have a thin seven-ply shell with a Michigan gumwood core.

Drum designer John Good has given a lot of thought to the bearing edge. He wanted an edge that could respond to high tuning without choking, whilst remaining noticeably resonant despite the muffling quality of heavier 'jazz' die-cast counter hoops. The edge is known as the Jazz Series 'Butter Edge'. The shells have no reinforcement hoops. This creates a less focussed sound, but one that helps the instrument resonate as a whole. All the shells are also timbre-matched as a set for optimal compatibility.

The combination of a slightly rounder bearing edge, die-cast counter hoops, STM (suspension tom mounts) and coated DW heads gives these drums their distinct sound.

Unique to DW's drum kits are its specialised shell configuration (SSC), which allows the customer to choose between X, VLT (vertical low timbre) or VLX shells for a unique sound.

John and his business partner always admired the Gretsch sound but wanted to take it a step further, and were able to blend maple and gumwood together to create this kit's particular sound. John says: 'With the Gretsch style thing we're using thin plies, 1/36in maple, gum, maple and so on, and they're very thin plies of gum. What I wanted to do is take my 1/36 and a seven-ply shell and go two maple, three gum and two maple. But the gum in the core of the shell is 1/20in think to accentuate the properties of it in between the maple. And what you get is a really nice attack with a beautiful "wow" from the maple, and a nice soft, round, resonant sound from the gum.'

■ There are eight lugs per head. The hoops and heads are tensioned with substantial metal claws. These are internally felt-cushioned and utilise standard square-head tension bolts.

■ The individual lugs are all locking washer-secured, just as the snare.

■ The batter head bearing edge has a 60.5° internal angle just as the snare batter, with the external angle 'butter edge' slightly rounded to protect the head.

■ The shell thickness is 7.6mm including the internal and external lacquer, but ably bears the weight of the mounted tom.

Bass drum

20in x 16in, weight 11.5kg (including damping pillow).

■ The bass drum's 42mm wooden hoops are satin pearl-covered on the outside and maple on the inside. The seven-ply appears to be the same as that used for the drum shells. The wrap overlap is cleanly executed but represents an uncharacteristically crude solution; I suggest something more elegant would complement the rest of the drum.

■ The supplied heads are single-ply coated DW Remos with a traditional non-ported resonant. The heads feature Remo's standard, glued-channel aluminium flesh hoop.

■ The drum has the serial 12603 and the badge has a single 7mm port.

■ The bass drum has two substantial and adjustable 37cm legs. These revolve through 180°, extend with a drum key lock, and have optional and micro-adjustable rubber feet or spikes.

■ Internally the drum has cushion resonance damping similar to the Evans type, secured with straps and Velcro. The fundamental timbre of the pristine shell is D.

■ The drum has a Krupa-style cymbal mount for that important little splash. This mount is sturdy and almost infinity adjustable, not to be confused with any 1950s abominations. Internally the mount is secured with two No 2 Phillips bolts.

■ The drum also has a 'banana' mount for the tom – this nod to the classic Ludwig mount irons out all the engineering wrinkles and works without risk of blood-blistered fingers! The mount is very securely fixed internally with two 0.5in nuts, spring washers and 2in load washers. In practice the adjustment is still a little fiddly and though delightfully retro isn't really ideal.

Tom 1

12in x 8in, weight 4.5kg. Serial No 12601. The stick included for scale in the overhead shot on page 135 is a 7A.

Note that the single 'rack' tom has a DW STM RIMS-like mount coupled to a bass-drum slide track similar to the old Ludwig design. DW offer both the slide track BDM and vintage-style rail mount. The slide track BDM is available in single- and double-tom configurations in Chrome, Satin Chrome, Black Nickel, Black Chrome, and 24 Karat Gold finishes. The rail mount is available in a single-tom configuration and Chrome. So no need to lug around extra tom stands! These mounts have been engineered to have the least possible stress and sonic effect on the bass drum. There are no huge holes in the top of the shell.

■ The steel STM ring is carefully isolated from the shell with four rubber rings that only contact the DW lugs. The mount itself is further rubber isolated.

■ All the tom hoops are the same cast and chromed type as the snare, with six lugs per head on this drum, and all the tuning bolts have the standard square head.

■ The shell is 7.5mm thick (custom to this drum), perfectly round and the interior clear-lacquered and pitched at G#.

■ The resonant 45.7° and batter bearing 46.6° edges are interesting – deeply cut on the inside and a very slight rounding to the peak. These customised bearing edges are intentional and all part of the DW philosophy – every drum is different.

■ The heads are both vintage-style single-ply coated DW Remos. Each head has six lugs.

Tom 2

14in x 14in, weight 6kg including legs. Serial No 12602. This is constructed exactly as tom 1, with eight lugs per head and the same head configuration. The batter bearing edge comes in at 45.2° and the resonant at 46°. The fundamental shell timbre is Eb. The suspension is via three traditional but very light shell-mounted legs with integral memory locks and interesting two-stage feet.

Signed off

This is probably the best-made kit I've ever seen. It represents a serious pro kit from a company with 30-plus years of experience in keeping drummers working. I can see many busy session and jazz drummers enjoying this kit for it's no-nonsense quality and simplicity. This is only one of five major types of DW kit, all infinitely variable in detail.

Tama 'Silverstar'
VK 52KSBCM

This Tama kit represents the 'bread and butter' arena for the busy gigging drummer. Affordable and fairly rugged, this kit will survive the rigours of small pub and club gigs and produce a decent sound.

Tama history

Hoshino Gakki began manufacturing drums in 1965 under the name 'Star Drums'. The founder's Hoshino surname translates as 'star field', and 'Star' continues to be used in the names of Tama drums. The drums were originally manufactured at Hoshino's subsidiary, Tama Seisakusho. The two upmarket lines, 'Imperial Star' and 'Royal Star', were introduced to the American market and were successful and more affordable compared to the more expensive American-made drums offered by Rogers, Ludwig and Slingerland.

In 1974 Hoshino decided to make a concerted effort to produce high-quality drums and hardware and start marketing its drums under the Tama brand. Tama was the name of the owner's wife, and means 'jewel' in Japanese. Many Tama drums are now made at the Guangzhou Hoshino factory in China.

Made in China in 2011

Condition on arrival

This is a new kit straight from the factory and kindly supplied by Martin Holland-Lloyd of Rattle & Drum, Derby, England. R&D offer a well-stocked drum department and friendly service uncommon in a world of Internet dealings.

Getting up and running

This noticeably lightweight kit arrived assembled and is supplied complete with Tama hardware. For the purposes of assessment the kit was trialled with a set of Zildjian 'A' customs.

General description

The kit comprises a modern drum arrangement: two mounted toms, an unusual size floor tom, a wooden snare and a 22in bass drum. The shells are birch ply. The finish is Blue Chameleon sparkle, though the kit is currently also available in seven other finishes. Both wraps and lacquers are available.

The snare

14in x 5in, weight 3kg. This six-ply snare has a Tama 'Powercraft 2' coated batter and a thin clear snare head. The coated batter has a very good brush surface. The snare has eight tension rods per head sharing a common low mass 'bridge'-type lug for minimal shell damping.

■ The 6mm shell has the current Tama signature badge.

■ The snare has a 45° inside bearing edge, but unlike the Pearl edge this is softened considerably by an exterior rounding, contributing to a sound that requires less damping of the high harmonics.

■ A nice touch is the very gentle, almost imperceptible slope towards the snare beds on the resonant bearing edge – this should make it easier to achieve even tensioning of the resonant head.

■ The eight individual lugs have no isolator just a simple washer secured with a No 1 Phillips. These small lugs are newly designed for the Silverstar series, reducing the surface area the lugs occupy on the shell, which will encourage more shell resonance.

■ The Gladstone-style snare mechanism is a well-engineered and sprung throw release. The snares are tensioned with black polyester ribbon through the 20 steel strands. Fine adjustment is via a plastic knurled thumbscrew.

■ The snares superficially resemble the Puresound type.

■ The rims are triple-flanged chrome with stainless steel 0.2in tension bolts; these have standard metal washers. The bolt thread is a standard modern 3/16in–24G. Be aware, however, that bolt lengths vary from drum to drum.

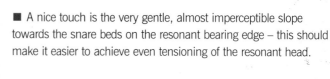

■ The interior stamp declares the Guangzhou Hoshino origin of the all birch shells.

■ As you might expect, this snare sounds very lively and 'open' with a lot of shell resonance. The brash quality may need a little taming for many uses.

Hardware

The supplied hardware is Tama 'Roadpro'.

■ Tom bracket
Weight 1.75kg. Lightweight but inspiring confidence – you get the sense they'd survive local gigs, and they offer versatile positioning. They have drum-key adjustable memory locks and a ball-joint swivel.

■ Snare stand
Weight 3.25kg (fairly standard). This stable triple-braced stand features a wing-nut tilting system for adjustable snare drum placement, and adjustable cradle grips. The floor tripod has the usefully small footprint essential with today's multiple pedal rigs.

■ Cymbal boom stand
Weight 4kg.

The telescopic knurled cymbal arm allows for a useful amount of positioning possibilities. The cymbal arm can naturally also fit back inside the main pipe tube, converting to a straight cymbal stand. This is a sleek, versatile, substantial stand and very light for a triple brace. The cymbal retainer has a useful quick-release feature.

Two similar stands are supplied with the kit, one with, the other without a boom facility, and with little difference in weight.

■ Hi-hat stand
Weight (minus cymbals) 4kg.

Be aware the triple-leg stand may hinder a double bass pedal arrangement.

The double chain-style link has a useful direct vertical pull. There's some scope for adjusting the torque of the pedal action. This is a bit 'plasticky' but will be OK for light use.

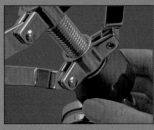

■ Single bass drum pedal
Weight 2kg. A basic pedal with single chain drive. The adjustable beater length and 'power glide' requires a standard drum key. The single-spring tension adjustment is via two knurled finger locks.

■ Cymbals
These were supplied by Headstock Distribution for this case study and are not part of the kit! But they're a great complement to the kit in a rock context. (For more on these cymbals see page 60.) They comprise a 14in Zildjian A Custom Mastersound hi-hat; a 16in Zildjian A Custom crash; and a 22in Zildjian Rock Ride Z3.

The bottom cymbal tilt mechanism is a spring-loaded plastic screw type. Matt Nolan custom hi-hats not included!

The foot-base has two adjustable spikes. These may require a No 2 Phillips.

■ The bass drum has two substantial 35cm adjustable legs. These revolve through 360° and have optional and adjustable rubber feet or spikes.

■ The drum has a sturdy fixing for the sliding twin-tom mount at the front top of the shell. Internally the mount has a lightweight plate to avoid tearing the shell. This is secured and tightened with a No 1 Phillips. Note again the stronger diagonal shell join.

Bass drum
22in x 18in, weight 11.5kg.

■ The bass drum's wooden hoops have eight art deco influenced rubber-lined claw hooks per head and utilise standard square-head tension bolts. There are eight corresponding *individual* low mass lugs per head.

Toms 1 and 2
Tom 1 (10in x 8in, weight 2.75kg) and tom 2 (12in x 9in, weight 3.25kg) are both attached directly to the bass drum with substantial and adjustable mounts and the 'Star-Mount' suspension system, a version of the RIMS approach.

■ The supplied heads are Tama, with integral twin-ply damping rings that extend only 5.5cm into the main head. The front head is a textured off-white and the batter clear; there is currently no port in the resonant head.

■ The seven-ply shell thickness is a thin 7.3mm including the internal lacquer and external wrap. The bearing edge is a steep 35° and very rounded on the outer edge, the resulting sound further tempered by the fitted two-ply EQ-ring heads.

■ The Star-Mount has an unusual half-polyhedron shape which will be naturally less resonant than a round hoop – an interesting idea. This is fixed with a 4mm Allen wrench and a 10mm ring spanner.

■ The suspension system is free-mounted on the lug bolts. The clamps are secured with an accessory-type ringed wing bolt.

■ The Star-Mount system was developed by Tama to free the resonance of their drum shells. This new mounting system provides support at four points on the batter-side hoop. The bracket eye-bolts slide to the left and right, so it's possible to prevent the eye-bolts from touching each other even when setting up two toms close to each other.

The MTH905N double-tom holder for the Silverstar series also makes it possible to move toms forward or backward up to 50mm to any position, simply by loosening a square-headed bolt.

■ The six small individual lugs per head are lightweight and the tuning bolts have the standard square head.

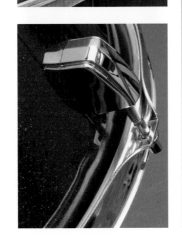

■ The six-ply shells are 5.9mm thick and the interior is lacquered. The resonant and batter bearing edges are 45° interior with a shallower cut external 45°, resulting in a sharp head contact and some signs of economy.

■ There's also some subtle bubbling in the wrap on the middle tom.

■ Both heads are clear single-ply Powercraft 2s.

Tom 3

16in x 14in, weight 5.5kg.

■ The heads, rims, shells and bearing edge of this floor tom follow the pattern of the two mounted toms, though there are eight lugs.

■ The leg lugs are low mass pattern and have no memory locks. The three 1.25kg legs have substantial finger screws setting the heights plus basic rubber feet.

Signed off

This is a fine-sounding kit that would see any drummer through a first series of semi-pro gigs. The hardware is very light but appropriate for purpose. The heads are OK and work, though I suspect many drummers will opt to change to Remo or Evans.

Roland TD-12KX: V-stage series

This pro kit comprises five very responsive and drum-like trigger pads, three rubber cymbal triggers and a complex three-way hi-hat trigger.

All the 'drums' feel great, with none of that dead practice-pad dullness of early electronic kits. This is achieved by a combination of real Remo mesh heads that are tensioned acoustic-style, and rubber-coated metal hoops that produce responsive rimshots. All the triggers have some degree of dynamic response.

Digital developments

I remember a time in the 1980s when it seemed the acoustic drum kit was approaching extinction. I worked then as a sound engineer, recording such acts as Duran Duran and Yazoo. Recording sessions that had previously involved real people pouring their hearts and souls into instruments were turning into 'data transfer' operations, as SMPTE timecode and MIDI interfaces bleeped and crashed. Complex cymbal sounds were replaced by rhythmic flashes of white noise, and bass drums became a transient electric click. The Simmons Kit and the Linn computer seemed to rule the airwaves.

Thankfully, though many of the people were fooled for some of the time, the old truism prevailed and the acoustic kit soon enjoyed a happy renaissance.

The subtleties of an organic instrument are hard to beat – ask any acoustic *guitarist*. However, the electric guitar in the hands of a genius musician *has* developed a complex ethereal language of its own. I predict a parallel relationship in percussion, where certain songs will lend themselves to acoustic nuances and others to the dramatic and extended palette of ever more complex digital samples. Perhaps drummers will change instrument mid-set, just as guitarists switch to unplugged for a dramatic change of perspective. To some extent this digital co-existence already happens, but with the quality now available this practice deserves a shift to the mainstream.

Heads

The Roland engineers derived their mesh-head ideas from observing a child's trampoline. Mr Kakehashi, the founder of Roland, introduced the developers to Remo Belli, the founder of Remo, who have 50 years' experience with synthetic drumheads.

Everyone agrees the more common rubber pad is too solid and not so good for drummer's wrists. The 'trampoline' mesh gives a better and also adjustable feel. The head is two-ply, with a patented 45° crossover.

Hi-hat

■ The good news is that you use your own preferred hi-hat stand and bass drum pedal, and the hi-hat pedal can be switched to become a second bass drum when required. The hi-hat 'pair' – the VH11 – is actually one closed unit that 'chicks' against a sophisticated motion sensor sitting on the lower cymbal cup. The hi-hat also has two twin-channel outputs giving six sounds – closed, open, top 'ride', side 'ride' and foot-operated 'clash' and 'chick'. It made me revaluate how complex the variety and blend of sounds are from the simple hi-hat.

■ According to Roland the motion sensor sits in the centre of the bottom pad, and they decided to use a spring to push down the sensor to send the open/closed information to the sound module. They'd previously tried many mechanical structures, including optical types.

Drums

The lower two of the 'drums' – currently PD105s – have 'snare' potential, though all the pads have a slight acoustic snare rattle, which is not distracting, adding an interesting acoustic transient to practice use. These 10in x 3.5in 105s

are used for the main snare and tom 3. The shells are made of Acousticon, a multi-ply compressed paper produced by Remo in the USA. This is a good environmentally friendly wood saving.

■ A second 8in x 2.25in set of smaller 'drums' – the PD85s – are designated toms 1 and 2. These are shell-less, almost like a roto tom.

■ The rubber CY12 R/C 'cymbals' are reassuringly heavy and have two twin-channel outputs for ride, and crash triggers, 'bell' sounds and cymbal rolls are all possible.

■ The 12in x 3.5in Acousticon KD20 'bass drum' is mounted on a sturdy quad set-up and you use the supplied Roland beater with your own favourite pedal (or in my case this beat up Pearl).

is a factor. This set-up seems to lend itself to a semi-permanent rig, as in a teaching environment, theatre pit or practice room, not a quick gig down the local bar! A busy drum tech would need to be very careful with the internal loom wiring, as this could easily be torn at the exposed junctions. Positioning options are very versatile with lots of Swiv-O-Matic ball joints and boom arms.

Control unit

■ The heart of the rig is the TD12 Percussion sound module. This offers a menu-driven choice of kits from small birch samples to huge maple bass drums, as well as lots of reverb options and a group mixer, giving quick tweaks to relative levels of groups

such as crash and toms as well as individual bass drum, hi-hat and snare. All the sounds have edit options, and customised settings can be stored so you can create your own maple and birch custom kit at whatever shell size you like.

Rack

■ The whole kit is mounted on a fairly rugged collapsible drum rack. However, the first assembly of this rig from shipping cartons took me a day, frustrated by a lack of co-ordinated rig instructions; there are currently four separate sets of diagrams and 'Japalese' text. None of this pointed out the critical nature of the orientation of the internal electrical looms – a very frustrating experience. With familiarity and a sensible part de-rig I think you could get the rig down to an hour, which is still twice as long as an acoustic kit, so that

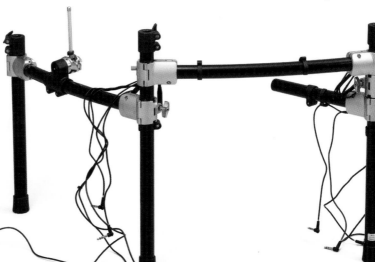

Sound

The Roland sounds excellent and the versatility is astonishing. How useful it could be in a pit-orchestra gig to be able to offer a sexy little Gretsch kit for a swing number then switch to a mighty 24in bass drum and concert toms for a Queen anthem!

It's also very useful to have all the Latin 'toys' available with a conventional kit technique alongside three timpani for a novelty effect – great for a pantomime/comedy gig. Roland also offer a nod to rock history with very convincing samples of classic Simmons SDS5s and TR808s for those retro moments.

All stick and beater gauges are perceived by the sensors as equal, so intriguingly a lambswool beater on a cymbal still sounds like hickory. Oh well, come the next software...

Playability

With most sticks the kit is actually easier to play than a conventional kit due to the extra bounce afforded by the mesh heads and the foam-covered piezo that supports the centre of the heads, all combined with the compact nature of the layout – a boon for beginners. Practicing with cans means there are no anti-social behaviour issues! Beware if using this kit for practice then performing on an acoustic kit live that the acoustic kit is going to be much harder work!

There is also a 'brushes' programme which only works with the coarse plastic brush type – this would be OK for occasional non-serious use, but purists would have reservations. This is clearly a complex area for a digital trigger.

Maintenance

Roland recommends tensioning and replacing the heads much as a normal kit. However, the set-up for the head doesn't change the amplified pitch, just the 'feel' or stick rebound of the

head. Removing the head on the 'snare' reveals the centrally mounted top 'cone' piezo transducer (head sound) and flat lower transducer (rim sound). The sensor is a normal piezo-pickup, but the cone-shaped cushion has a four-ply structure with differing hardness/softness of cushioning to optimise the vibration from the drum-head to the piezo-sensor.

The compressed paper shell is seamless, and I'm sure this very drumlike structure contributes to the realistic end sound. The bearing edge for the head, however, is ultimately the moulded plastic of the transducer frame.

When tensioning a replacement head Roland recommend a 7mm gap between the hoop and the frame. In practice the factory settings had 13.3mm of thread revealed above the lugs, which worked well.

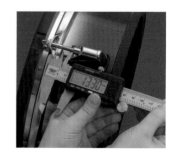

Amplification

Roland recommend a substantial monitor wedge for the LF component of the drums range and two small 'nearfield' monitors for the HF

spectrum. These work well, though without the sheer dynamic impact of an acoustic kit at close quarters. However, I'm sure anybody interested in using an electronic kit in a stadium rock context could arrange all the wedges and bass bins needed to achieve this effect and, unfortunately, its associated tinnitus.

Ancillaries

This specific Roland offers much more than just an electronic kit. It has sophisticated sequencer functions, record and playback, click track etc, as well as good EQ compression and reverb. Each drum sound can also be modified changing the size and type of shell and the head type, so this is like buying 50 kits and then mixing and matching them to your individual requirements.

Useful applications

■ Yamaha DD65

In the electronic arena Yamaha offer not only centre-stage equivalents to the Roland but also much more humble but very valid 'practice pad'-based systems such as the DD45 and DD65. The DD65 has foot pedals for the bass drum and hi-hat. Through a good PA these apparently simple devices produce very convincing sounds, and in a practice situation they provide a noise-free and dynamically sensitive facility. These are great for group teaching, especially with their headphones and record facility. The electronics include a series of play-along tracks for tuition use. Excellent, and more fun than a practice pad.

■ Jobeky

An interesting recent development arises from many drummers' rejection of the aesthetics of the 'skeletal' nature of electronic kits – the top-of-the-line Roland has now become more drum-like, and British manufacturer Jobeky make kits that look acoustic but are really trigger mechanisms for Roland modules.

■ Aquarian

As more drummers attach triggers to their drum shells, head manufacturer Aquarian are developing heads with built-in triggers; now that could be a real breakthrough – acoustic feel and responses but with all the advantages of easy amplification and digital trigger samples. Artist relations director Chris Brady tells me: 'The inHEAD uses a force sensing resistor. There are no wires. This head doesn't use Piezo pickups. The trigger is inked on to the head. The conductive material is suspended in the ink.' Watch this space!

Pearl VBX
'Vision Birch'

Every drummer
needs a simple,
solid, reliable kit with
a versatile sound. Over
the last thirty years, Pearl
has carved a niche for itself
in this area. This is the kit
that could get you from bar
gig to stardom without
changing the heads.

Pearl history

Founded by Katsumi Yanagisawa, who began
manufacturing music stands in Sumida, Tokyo,
in April 1946, the Pearl Musical Instrument
Company is now a multinational corporation
based in Japan, with a wide range of products,
predominantly percussion. Drum manufacture
started in 1950. In 1966 Pearl introduced
its first professional drum kit, the 'President
Series'. For a time in the early 1970s Pearl
was distributed in the US by Norlin, the then
parent company of Gibson guitars.

Condition on arrival

This is a new kit straight from the factory, supplied by Andy Payne, who recommends this as 'a good first serious working kit'. The Vision VBX is Pearl's most affordable 100% birch drum set. Birch has long been recognised for its focussed, naturally EQ'd sound. The VBX comes with professional two-ply batter heads, and a steel 'SensiTone' snare drum.

Getting up and running

The kit arrived assembled by Birmingham Drum Centre and is supplied complete with Pearl 900 Series hardware. For the purposes of assessment the kit was trialled with a set of Zildjian 'A' Customs.

General description

The kit comprises a modern drum arrangement – two mounted toms and one floor tom, a metal snare and a 22in bass drum. The shells are 100% birch, apart from the snare. The higher drums are six-ply and the lower ones eight-ply. The significance of this is summed up by Pearl's European branding manager Jeroen Breider: 'It is much easier to get a good volume out of the smaller toms; by comparison the bigger drums, like floor toms and bass drums, have relatively lower volume. To compensate for this the lower VBX drums are made thicker, as the thicker the drums the louder they get. This aids an overall balanced volume around the kit.'

The finish is clear birch, though the kit is currently also available in Ruby Fade, Black Ice, Concord Fade and Orange Zest.

Newer versions of this kit dubbed the VBL don't have six or eight ply differences between shells, though this feature is retained on the Reference series drums.

Made in China in October 2010. Shown with an additional Eddie Ryan wooden snare.

The snare

14in x 5.5in, weight 3.75kg. The SensiTone snare has a Pearl Protone-coated batter and a thin clear snare head. The coated batter has a very good brush surface. Pearl are one of a handful of manufacturers not using Remo heads, and their own heads have a distinct character designed to complement the drum design.

The snare has eight tension rods per head sharing a common 'bridge' lug for minimal shell damping.

■ The precision-contoured lever allows for a fast and absolute on/off function. A large adjustment knob enables fine-tuning.

■ The rims are triple-flanged chrome with stainless steel 0.2in tension bolts. These have standard metal washers. The bolt thread is a standard modern 3/16in–24G and the lugs have a brass swivel nut – brass to stainless steel will naturally bind, avoiding de-tensioning.

■ The snare has a sharp 45° bearing edge, contributing to the very bright cutting sound.

■ The outer steel 1mm shell has the Pearl signature badge.

■ The snare mechanism is a well-engineered and sprung throw release and the snares are tensioned with mylar strips through the 20 steel strands. The fine adjustment is via a substantial well-knurled thumbscrew.

■ The snares themselves superficially resemble a Puresound type.

■ The eight individual lugs with isolator and locking nut all have substantial locking washers secured with a No 2 Phillips. The internal design is very well thought through.

■ This snare sounds very bright, and for me needs a little calming of the high harmonics, which isn't difficult. See page 41.

Hardware

All the stands are from Pearl's own 900 series and include integral memory locks. The 900 is Pearl's affordable mid-price series.

Tom arms

These manage to be lightweight whilst inspiring confidence – you get the sense they would survive a semi-pro tour, and they offer fairly versatile positioning.

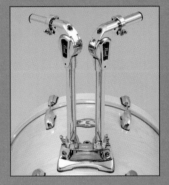

Snare stand

Weight 3.25kg. This stable triple-braced stand features a Uni-Lock tilting system for infinitely adjustable drum placement, and highly adjustable cradle grips. The floor tripod has a usefully small footprint, essential with today's multiple-pedal rigs.

Cymbal boom stand

Weight 4.5kg. The BC-900 is a member of the MIPA award-winning 900 series hardware family, and features a Uni-Lock Tilter for infinitely adjustable cymbal positioning. The telescopic knurled cymbal arm allows for an incredible amount of positioning possibilities. The cymbal arm can also fit back inside the main pipe tube, converting to a straight stand. This is a sleek and versatile stand and not *too* heavy.

Hi-hat stand

Weight (minus cymbals) 4.5kg. This features parallel Sure Struts that resist lateral twisting to prevent squeaks and instability.

A strong chain-style link has a direct vertical pull.

There's considerable scope for adjusting the torque of the pedal action.

The bottom cymbal tilt mechanism is a simple spring-loaded screw type.

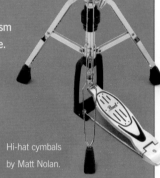

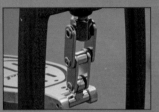

Hi-hat cymbals by Matt Nolan.

Single bass drum pedal

Weight 2.75kg. The P-900 has a linear round cam, single chain-drive. Patented 'Power-Shifter' adjustments shift the pedal back and forth, thus changing the angle of the chain-drive and affecting the 'feel' of the pedal. This is accomplished with a standard drum key. The adjustable beater angle requires a 3mm Allen wrench. The spring-tension adjustment is via two knurled finger locks.

Cymbals

The cymbals shown were supplied by Headstock Distribution for this case study. They comprise a 14in Zildjian A Custom Mastersound hi-hat; a 16in Zildjian A Custom crash; and a 22in Zildjian Rock Ride Z3. These are a great complement to the kit in a rock context. For more on these great cymbals see page 61.

■ The individual lugs are all locking washer secured and cushioned as the snare.

■ The shell thickness is a substantial 10.6 mm including the internal and external lacquer and appears to be eight-ply. The Pearl label tells us: 1 2 B E, the figures 1 2 indicating 2010 and the letters B E indicating October.

■ The bearing edge is again a sharp 45°, – the resulting bright sound tempered by the fitted two-ply EQ-ring heads.

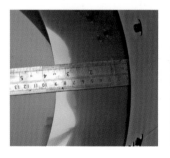

Bass drum
22in x 18in,
weight 13kg.

■ The bass drum's wooden hoops have eight rubber-lined claw hooks per head.

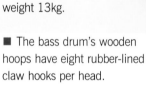

■ The bass drum has two substantial and adjustable legs. These revolve through 180°, extend, and have optional and adjustable rubber feet or spikes.

■ There are eight *individual* cushioned 'bridge' lugs per head. These are also cushioned from the hoops and utilise standard square-head tension bolts.

■ The heads are Pearl Protones with integral twin-ply damping rings that extend 9cm into the main head. The front head is in ebony and the batter clear. There is currently no port in the resonant head. The batter hoop has a non-slip pedal grip/hoop protector.

■ The drum has a sturdy 'bridge-style' twin-tom mount at the centre top of the shell. Internally the mount has a substantial but lightweight plate to avoid tearing the shell. This is secured and tightened with a No 2 Phillips.

Toms 1 and 2

Tom 1 (10in x 8in, weight 3.25kg) and tom 2 (12in x 9in, weight 4kg) are both attached directly to the bass drum with substantial and adjustable mounts and the Pearl Optimount suspension system, a version of the RIMS approach. Pearl deserve a lot of credit for this low-mass easy to fit rim mount, which can be off and on in seconds using just a simple drum key.

■ The six individual bridge lugs per head are substantial and isolated by soft plastic mounts, the tuning bolts have the standard square head.

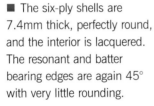

■ The six-ply shells are 7.4mm thick, perfectly round, and the interior is lacquered. The resonant and batter bearing edges are again 45° with very little rounding.

■ The heads are Protone clears, oil-filled, with an integral perimeter EQ ring, two-ply batter and a clear single-ply resonant.

■ The integrated suspension system is clamped to the rims rather than the lug bolts. The clamps are secured with a regular modern drum key.

Tom 3

14in x 14in, weight 5.25kg.

■ The heads, rims, shells and bearing edge of this floor tom follow the pattern of the two mounted toms, except that the larger tom is eight-ply, though no thicker. The scarf joint provides 80% greater surface area than conventional butt joints. Pearl claim this provides extra strength and integrity to the shell while simultaneously eliminating air pockets that can disrupt vibration.

■ The leg lugs are bridge pattern and have no memory locks. The legs have substantial finger screws setting the heights and rubber 'air suspension' feet.

Signed off

This is a good-sounding, well-made kit that would see any drummer through that first series of gigs. The six/eight-ply approach is a luxury at the price and makes good sense. The hardware is also very slick and fit for purpose. The heads are OK and work well – on the bass drum particularly – though I suspect many drummers will opt to change to Evans or Remos.

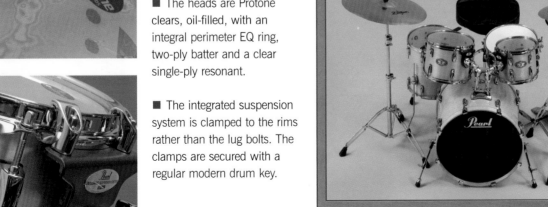

Gretsch USA
American custom

During my
17-year
stint in the studio,
I heard a lot of kits,
and none recorded better
than Gretsch. Listen
to any Rolling Stones
album for a great,
simple
Gretsch groove.

Friedrich Gretsch

The Gretsch Manufacturing
Company was founded in
1883 by Friedrich Gretsch,
a migrant to the US from
Germany, who soon started
manufacturing banjos,
tambourines and drums. In
1895 Friedrich Gretsch died
at the age of 39 and the
emerging company was taken
over by his son, Fred. By 1916
the company had moved into
a large ten-storey building in
Brooklyn, New York. Their
drum kits are regarded as the
greatest recording kits in the
world, and have also been
extremely popular with most
of the world's jazz players.
The company is now affiliated
to the Fender group.

Condition on arrival

This is another brilliant kit found at the Birmingham Drum Centre, though this one is actually owned by MD Chris Payne. The finish is a one-off Vintage Oyster with an aqua blue cast.

There are no cymbals as supplied – at this level we all want our own cymbals. Those illustrated here are two brilliant and innovative cymbals from British custom maker Matt Nolan and my 'splash' and China from Istanbul. The heads are Gretsch Permatone by Remo, which are standard to this kit. The sticks shown for scale are 7As.

Getting up and running

The drums are supplied fully assembled, and about ten minutes should see it fully rigged with the memory locks set for future gigs. The tuning is currently a low rock pitch throughout, with a rich resonant response from the toms.

Gretsch USA American custom Assembled in the USA from US and imported components

General description

The kit comprises a classic four-drum arrangement – one stand-mounted tom, one floor tom, a snare and a bass drum. All the hardware is an optional extra; here I'm using three DW 9000 cymbal stands, a hi-hat and twin bass-drum pedals, and one DW 7000 stand. Gretsch traditionally dominated the smaller jazz kit arena, but this custom kit is more versatile with a deeper bass drum and snare.

The Gretsch USA Custom series is hand-crafted in Ridgeland, USA. The six-ply shell is the cornerstone of the legendary Gretsch sound. The drums have traditional Gretsch silver sealer die-cast hoops.

This kit can be supplied in any Gretsch finish.

The snare

14in x 6.5in, weight 4.75kg. The snare has a single-ply Gretsch USA coated batter and a thin, milky clear Permatone resonant head with a generous ten individual tension rods per head.

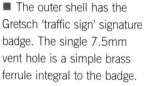

■ The 20 distinctive Gretsch lugs are very substantial and each bolt has one chromed steel washer.

■ The tuning bolts require a 0.2in square drum key for tuning. The bolt thread is the common 3/16in–24G.

■ The lug thread inserts also have an internal nylon bushing to further prevent rattle and slippage. Gretsch are naturally serious about a good rattle-free drum.

■ The six-ply shell is perfectly round and 13 7/8in diameter, bearing edge to bearing edge.
Note the wrap doesn't extend into the hoop area, freeing the shell and leaving the head unimpeded.

■ The outer shell has the Gretsch 'traffic sign' signature badge. The single 7.5mm vent hole is a simple brass ferrule integral to the badge.

■ The hoops are die-cast as standard on all Gretsch drums. Their extra weight naturally gives the drum more attack and possibly less sustain.

■ The inner shell is unobstructed and silk lacquer coated. The shell thickness is a thin 7.89mm, excluding the wrap. There is an almost invisible straight seam in the ply.

160

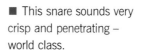

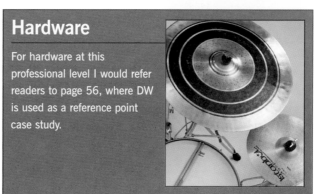

■ The shell is model number C-657Y215 and serial number 69681.

■ The snare-head side of the shell has a bearing edge with a rounded 61° angle on the inside edge and a soft curve on the outer edge, all contributing to the sound of the drum. There's also a very broad snare-bed indentation encompassing almost an eighth of the drum's circumference at both snare junctions, visible against a straight edge.

■ The lugs all have substantial locking washers secured with a 7mm socket wrench.

■ The snare comes with Gretsch-branded 50mm wide 20-strand single-course steel wires. The snares are coarse-tensioned with a standard drum key and strip of clear plastic. The snares have chromed end plates and the fine adjustment is via an easily accessible thumbscrew. This also has a neat bullet throw-off for 'no snare' sounds. Conveniently the throw-off lever revolves to a range of positions through 180°.

■ This snare sounds very crisp and penetrating – world class.

■ The batter-head bearing edge is similar but without the snare bed. As found, some sawdust was interfering with the bearing edge but this was easily cleaned.

■ The snare mechanism is secured on the throw-off side with a 5/16in socket wrench and on the 'fixed' side with a No 2 Phillips.

Hardware

For hardware at this professional level I would refer readers to page 56, where DW is used as a reference point case study.

■ Internally the drum has the model number G1822B, and the shell badge has a single 7.5mm port.

■ There are ten lugs per head. The hoops and heads are tensioned with substantial cast metal claws. These utilise standard square-head tension bolts.

■ The individual lugs are all internally locking washer secured just as the snare.

Bass drum

22in x 18in, weight 10kg, serial number 2008-0659.

■ The bass drum's 43.5mm wooden hoops are pearl-covered on the outside and matt black on the inside. The six-ply appears to be the same as that used for the drum shells. The wrap overlap is cleanly executed but represents a crude solution; something more elegant would complement the rest of the drum.

■ The batter head bearing edge has a 63.6° internal angle, with the external angle slightly rounded to protect the head.

■ The drum has no tom mount, leaving the shell free to resonate.

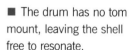

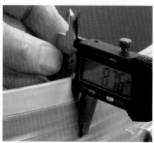

■ The shell thickness is 8.7mm, including the internal silver lacquer and external wrap.

■ The bass drum has two substantial and adjustable 36cm (max) legs. These revolve through 120°, extend with a thumbwheel lock and have optional and micro-adjustable rubber feet or spikes.

■ The supplied heads are single-ply Gretsch Permatones by Remo, with a traditional non-ported resonant head. The pinstripe batter head has an effective two-ply damping ring that brings out the fundamental nicely.

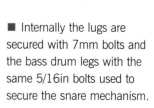

■ Internally the lugs are secured with 7mm bolts and the bass drum legs with the same 5/16in bolts used to secure the snare mechanism.

Tom 1

12in x 9in, weight 4.5kg (including RIMS attachment). Serial number 69682. Note that the single 'rack' tom has a Gretsch RIMS-like mount designed for coupling to any substantial tom stand. The RIM is designated 12 x 5 x 4 and the bracket 12-13, and is made in Taiwan. The rims are secured with a No 2 Phillips and a 3/8in socket.

■ The heavily chromed ring is carefully isolated from the shell with four rubber rings that only contact the cast hoops when suspended. The mount itself is further rubber-isolated from the external bracket.

■ The recommended tom stand is the DW 9000.

Tom 2

16in x 16in, weight 7kg (excluding legs). Serial number 20080661. This is constructed exactly as tom 1, with eight lugs per head and the same head configuration. The bearing edges are a consistent 60°. The suspension is via three traditional shell-mounted legs with no memory locks, a simple thumb lever and substantial rubber feet.

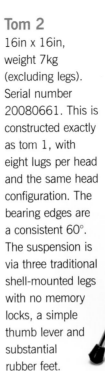

■ All the tom hoops are the same cast and chromed type as the snare, with five lugs per head on this drum. All the tuning bolts have the standard square head.

■ The shell model number G01925 is 6.8mm thick, perfectly round and the interior is silver-lacquered.

■ The resonant and batter bearing edges are a matching 60°.

■ The batter head is coated and the resonant a clear single-ply Permatone Remo.

Signed off

This is a serious and very attractive kit from a company with almost 130 years of experience in keeping pro drummers working. I can see both busy session and stage drummers enjoying this kit for its quality and simplicity – it also looks fantastic.

Yamaha
'Steve Gadd' kit

There may be '50 ways to leave your lover', but only one drummer who could conjure up such a tight groove from a simple military rudiment. This is the kit that Steve plays in Europe.

Steve Gadd

International session drummer Steve Gadd has been playing Yamaha drums since 1976. His name was for many years synonymous with the recording custom kit and the 9000, becoming the most popular professional kit in the world during the 1980s. Steve popularised small 10in toms and introduced floor tom-tom stands. He still likes birch tom-toms, but recently has preferred a maple bass drum. His 'Clapton' tour kit, featured here, comprises 22in x 14in maple Custom Absolute bass, 12in x 8in and 13in x 9in hanging toms, and 14in x 12in and 16in x 14in floor-mounted birch Custom Absolute toms. Other times he uses a small 10in x 7.5in tom, which he made famous in his studio days, and drops the 13in tom. For live work he prefers a high-steel 14in x 5.5in signature snare drum.

Getting up and running

The cymbals are a substitute 'K' Zildjian set, as Steve carries his favourites with him as he travels.

General description

The kit comprises a modern drum arrangement – two bass drum-mounted toms and two stand-mounted floor toms, a Steve Gadd custom snare and a maple bass drum. The finish is sprayed Piano Black lacquer.

YAMAHA

Made in Japan

The snare

14in x 5.5in. Serial number 0837. This now discontinued SD255SG snare is one of three Steve uses depending on the gig. Others have birch shells and wooden rims on a steel shell (as seen on the *Sessions For Robert* Eric Clapton DVD). It has a Remo 'Weatherking'-coated batter and a thin clear 'Weatherking' snare head with ten individual tension rods per head.

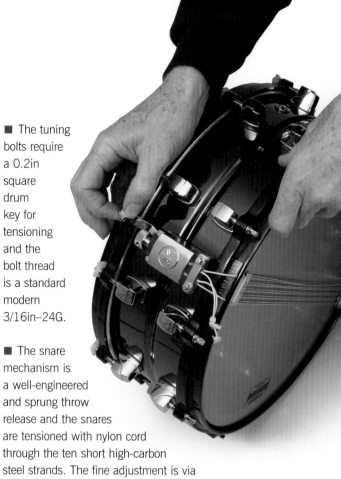

■ The tuning bolts require a 0.2in square drum key for tensioning and the bolt thread is a standard modern 3/16in–24G.

■ The snare mechanism is a well-engineered and sprung throw release and the snares are tensioned with nylon cord through the ten short high-carbon steel strands. The fine adjustment is via a substantial well-knurled thumbscrew.

■ The outer steel 1.2mm shell has the current Yamaha signature badge.

■ The 2.3mm rims are triple-flanged and black-chromed with 0.2in tension bolts. The 'stick-side' bolts have nylon tension retainers.

■ The snare has a 45° bearing edge.

■ The ten individual lugs are small body-high tension lugs with isolator and a non-locking nut.

■ All have substantial locking washers secured with a No 2 Pozidrive.

■ This snare sounds as you'd expect – solid, professional and versatile.

Hardware

All the stands are Yamaha except the hi-hat, which is DW. All have integral memory locks.

▪ Snare stand
This very stable triple-braced stand has a universal ball-joint cradle tilt and heavy-duty infinitely adjustable cradle grips. The floor tripod has a usefully small footprint.

▪ Cymbal boom stand
A versatile stand without being too heavy.

▪ Hi-hat stand
A DW 5000. Steve likes the feel of this, and Yamaha are currently working on a Yamaha Steve Gadd hi-hat with a similar response.

This two-legged version makes for easier positioning of the second bass-drum pedal. The legs also swivel for ultimate versatility.

The bottom cymbal tilt mechanism is a simple screw type.

▪ Bass drum pedals
Dual chain-drive and sturdy base plate with grip spurs. There is also the fully adjustable linkage to the second pedal and twin springs. Steve has a customised 'flat' on the main beater for better head contact.

All the pedals fit comfortably around the snare.

▪ Stick holder and metronome
Steve keeps careful tabs on tempos and feel with the help of a Tama rhythm watch.

▪ Music stand
This is illuminated and robust, with the Clapton set in the ring binder and his own custom brushes conveniently to hand. Steve likes his own Vic Firth custom sticks with wooden bead and lightly abraded for a better grip. We should all aspire to be this organised!

▪ Cymbals
According to Yard, Steve uses 14in Zildjian K Session hi-hat; 18in Zildjian K Constantinople crash; 18in Zildjian K Session Custom ride, and 16in Zildjian K Session Custom crash. He often uses a third riveted crash on his left.

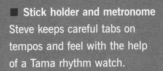

■ The individual lugs are all locking washer secured and cushioned as the snare.

■ The supplied heads are Remo-coated Ambassadors and Steve likes a lot of damping – a carefully folded house-removals blanket strapped into shape covers a third of both heads. There's a large port in the resonant head which is also used for microphone access.

Bass drum
22in x 14in.

■ The bass drum's wooden hoops have ten timpani handle tension rods.

■ There are ten *individual* cushioned lugs per head. As you might expect at this level, the hoops and heads are tensioned with substantial metal claws. These are also cushioned from the hoops.

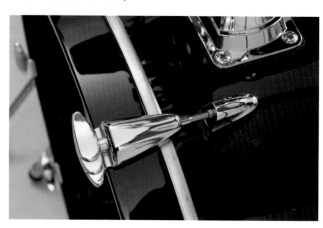

■ The bass drum has two substantial and adjustable legs. These revolve through 360°, extend and have optional and micro-adjustable rubber feet or spikes.

Toms 1 and 2

Tom 1 (12in x 8in) and tom 2 (13in x 9in) are both attached directly to the bass drum with substantial and adjustable ball-swivel mounts.

■ The black chrome rims are triple-flanged.

■ The six individual lugs per head are substantial and isolated by soft plastic mounts. The tuning bolts have the standard square head.

Tom 3 and Tom 4

Tom 3 is 14in x 12in, and tom 4 16in x 14in.

■ The heads, rims, shells and bearing edge of these floor toms follow the pattern of the two mounted toms.

■ The tom stand has substantial finger screws setting the heights and ball joints with memory locks secured with a standard key.

■ The shells are 6.52mm thick, perfectly round and the interior is black-lacquered.

■ The resonant and batter bearing edges are cut at 45°. The heads are a coated Ambassador batter and a clear Ambassador resonant.

■ The toms have a substantial mount attached to each shell.

Signed off

This kit reeks of a relaxed professionalism. No frills, just get down to it – the sort of groove machine that gives Steve what he needs to perform at his best. In the studio Steve occasionally dabbles with other kits when the gig calls for it.

Premier 'Elite' Gen-X maple and birch hybrid kit

The UK-based Premier company has had its share of ups and downs, but in 2011 bounced back with this serious pro-contender. The kit has style and individuality and deserves to succeed.

Condition on arrival

This is Premier's own demo kit and is in great condition apart from some head wear.

There are no cymbals supplied, as most pros would have that area covered. The heads are American Remos, which are standard to this kit.

Getting up and running

The drums are fully assembled and about 20 minutes should see it fully rigged with the memory locks set for future gigs. The tensioning is currently a bit random.

General description

The kit comprises a modern six-drum arrangement – two mounted toms, two floor toms, a snare and an extended bass drum. All the hardware is an optional extra; here I have two one-cymbal stands, a hi-hat and twin bass-drum pedals.

Gen-X is unique in offering a seven-ply shell combining both birch and maple in a researched ratio (two-ply birch on the outside and five-ply maple on the inside), potentially offering the key sonic features of the two. The same kit is also available completely in North American maple or birch if preferred.

There are 40 finishes on offer – vibrant woodgrain lacquers and lustrous sparkles in a combination of even-coat, fade or 'burst' applications.

A wide range of sizes is available as standard with the option of quick, standard, power or new short-stack toms to choose from. All sizes of bass drum are catered for, with or without a tom mount.

Made in Taiwan and assembled in the UK

The snare

14in x 5.5in, weight 4.5kg. The snare has a Premier-branded single-ply Remo 'Weatherking'-coated batter and a thin clear 'Weatherking' snare head with a generous ten tension rods per head.

■ The outer gloss-lacquered shell has the current pewter Premier signature badge.

■ The 20 full-width lugs are very substantial and cushioned from the shell with a soft black plastic Nyloc insert – this also extends into the lug to engage with the threads, to prevent detuning. The snare is the only drum in the kit without individual lugs for each head.

■ The lug thread inserts also have an internal nylon bushing to further prevent rattle and slippage. Clearly Premier are very serious about a good rattle-free recording kit.

■ The rims are cast low-profile steel Diamond chrome-plated with modern 'square' 0.2in tension bolts. In my experience the Premier Diamond chrome lasts for at least 50 years due to the complicated three-stage process of copper/nickel/chrome, with polishing after each plating. The drums are all available with triple-flanged pressed hoops on request. Each bolt has a steel washer.

■ The seven-ply shell is perfectly round and 13.75in diameter, bearing edge to bearing edge. All Premier drums are 3mm under standard size for a floating head effect, which makes for easier attuning.

■ The batter-head side of the shell has an interesting two-sided bearing edge with a rounded 125° angle on the outside edge and a soft curve based around 51° on the inner edge, contributing to the distinctive sound of the drum.

■ The inner shell is unobstructed and the shell thickness is a thin 6.1mm, including a coat of clear lacquer. Note the diagonal seams in the ply which improve the strength of the join.

■ The resonant head bearing edge is different again, with a more traditional one-sided but still rounded bearing based around 45°. There's a very subtle, almost imperceptible snare-bed indentation at both snare junctions, only visible against a straight edge.

■ The lugs all have locking washers secured with a No 2 Pozidrive. Ironically every screw was incredibly loose, possibly due to shrinkage in transport. Always check these before a recording.

■ The tuning bolts require a 0.2in square drum key for tuning and the bolt thread is a standard modern 3/16in–24G.

■ The 7.8mm vent hole is lined with a chrome nut and bolt (which can come loose causing an incredible rattle, so check this is secured internally; this requires a 17mm socket). This really needs a spring washer to avoid de-tensioning due to the vibration of playing.

■ This snare sounds as you'd expect – crisp and penetrating but also with a warmth that will see it sit well in the mix. World class.

■ The snare mechanism is a well-engineered and sprung throw release and the snares are tensioned with a strip of clear plastic looped through the 50mm wide 20-strand single-course steel wire snares. The snare tension is coarsely adjusted via four drum-key adjustable bolts (two per side) and the fine adjustment is via a thumbscrew.

■ There are ten individual cushioned lugs per head. As you might expect at this level, the hoops and heads are tensioned with substantial metal claws. These are also cushioned from the hoops and utilise standard square-head tension bolts.

■ The individual lugs are all locking washer secured and Nyloc cushioned, as the snare.

Bass drum
18in x 20in, weight 10kg.

■ The bass drum's 40mm wooden hoops are glitter-lacquered, one gold, one black. The seven-ply appears to be the same as that used for the shells.

■ The batter head bearing edge has the same 51° internal angle as the snare batter, with the external angle again approximating 120° (measured externally), both of these angles being slightly rounded to protect the head.

■ The shell thickness is 6.16mm including the internal and external lacquer, but this thin shell doesn't bear the weight of any mounted toms.

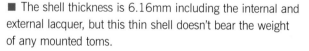

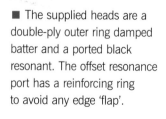

■ The supplied heads are a double-ply outer ring damped batter and a ported black resonant. The offset resonance port has a reinforcing ring to avoid any edge 'flap'.

■ The bass drum has two substantial and adjustable 40cm legs. These revolve through 360°, extend and have optional and micro-adjustable rubber feet or spikes.

Hardware

This all comes from the recommended 6000 series and all have integral memory locks.

■ Snare stand
Weight 3.75kg. For versatility this very stable triple-braced stand has a universal ball-joint cradle tilt and heavy-duty infinitely adjustable cradle grips.

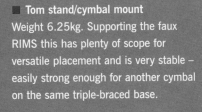

■ Tom stand/cymbal mount
Weight 6.25kg. Supporting the faux RIMS this has plenty of scope for versatile placement and is very stable – easily strong enough for another cymbal on the same triple-braced base.

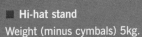

■ Cymbal boom stands
Weight 5.25kg each. A pro feature is the spring-loaded infinite position cymbal-tilter and 'disappearing' boom.

■ Hi-hat stand
Weight (minus cymbals) 5kg.

This features an easy to use locking variable tension adjuster, which gives a flexible choice of hi-hat response, a solid base plate and chain-drive, and Velcro and spike position stabilisers. On any decent drum mat this hi-hat will stay where it's put! The bottom cymbal tilt mechanism is also lockable for consistency of set-up.

■ Bass drum pedals
Weight 2.75kg (each). This has a dual chain-drive, dual-sided beaters, and a sturdy base plate with grip spurs and Velcro. There's also the fully-adjustable linkage to a second pedal, twin springs and all the necessary adjustment tools attached.

What to look for in a pro kit

A pro kit has to sound fantastic *every time*, whatever the gig or session. So:

- Consistent and easy tensioning is crucial. Fitted pro heads and tension-sustaining lugs are important.
- Your sound! – at this level the kit not only has to reflect *your* style and personality but has to be adaptable to the needs of the gig. Optional snare drums for different styles of song may be a factor.
- A fast double bass-drum pedal for complex bass rhythms may be essential.
- The stage appearance must be world class.
- You'd expect isolation mounts for the toms as standard at this price.
- The kit must be rugged enough to take a lot of punishment and suitable for the rigours of a world tour.
- The kit must be totally memory-locked for road crew pre-rigging.

The Premier Elite fits the bill.

- All the tom hoops are the same cast and chromed type as the snare, with six lugs per head on this drum. The lugs are substantial and isolated by soft plastic mounts. The tuning bolts have the standard square head.

- The shell is, as the snare, 5.7mm thick, perfectly round and the interior clear-lacquered with an offset join to the seven plies.

- The resonant and batter bearing edges are interesting – a deeply cut 46° on the inside and a shallow cut 46° on the outside, all slightly rounded off.

- The heads are a coated Ambassador batter and a clear Ambassador resonant.

Tom 1

9.75in x 7in, weight 3.5kg. The stick included in the picture for scale is a 7A. Note that the two suspended toms are flush-mounted in a 'RIMS-alike' isolated mount as now found on most pro kits.

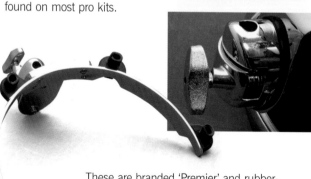

These are branded 'Premier' and rubber-isolated from the lugs. The substantial clamps are spring-loaded for a standard 10mm post.

Tom 2

12in x 8in, weight 4.25kg. This is constructed exactly as tom 1, with six lugs per head and the same head configuration, bearing edge and RIMS-like suspension.

Tom 3

14in x 12in, weight 5.5kg.

■ The heads, rims, 5.7mm shell and bearing edge of this small floor tom follow the pattern of the two mounted toms.

■ The three clamps securing the 10mm legs have rubber feet and the adjustable legs have an integral memory lock, conveniently tightened with a standard drum key.

Tom 4

16 x 14in, weight 7kg.

■ The rims and 5.7mm shell of this unusual floor tom follow the same pattern as the smaller one, with the same substantial clamps securing the 10mm legs.

■ Note that *all* the drum fittings – lugs and brackets – were a fraction loose, probably due to shrinkage in transport. It's worth checking all of these on any new kit before tensioning, as inevitably something will rattle and you may have wasted time attuning, followed by having to remove a head!

Stagg five-piece Student Series starter kit

Students need a good sound more than pros, as they need the positive feedback to sustain their youthful enthusiasm. So, it's great to hear that such a neat kit is available at a beginner's price. It looks fine and would certainly survive a few early gigs.

What to look for in a beginners' kit

You probably don't want to spend a fortune on a first kit, but in order to be useful a few simple factors are important:

- It must have a decent sound – if the kit sounds bad then all your efforts will be in vain and you'll give up.
- It must also look acceptable, as it takes up a lot of space in your home!
- It must be rugged enough to take a little punishment, even if it's not suitable for the rigours of a world tour.

The Stagg fits the bill.

Condition on arrival

The kit arrived in two cardboard boxes approximately 50–60cm square with the components neatly and efficiently packed for freight. The set-up is relatively simple: the two small toms and the snare are ready assembled, the bass drum and large tom are only missing one head, and all the shell-mounted lugs are fitted. All the heads are Chinese Remo.

Getting up and running

A couple of hours unpacking and assembling should do the trick.

General description

The kit comprises the classic post 1970s five drums – two mounted toms, a floor tom, a snare and a bass drum with six-ply all-basswood shells, finished here in natural but also available in Black, Wine Red, Pearl White, Pearl Black and Pearl Blue. There's one cymbal stand, a hi-hat and bass drum pedal.

Made in China, serial no
TIM 622L, total weight 46kg

The snare

14in x 5.5in, weight 3.25kg. The snare has a single-ply Remo UK textured batter and a thin clear snare head with eight individual tension rods per head.

■ The outer lacquered basswood shell is suitably badged with the current Stagg logo.

■ The rims are pressed triple-flanged steel, chrome-plated, with modern 'square' 0.2in tension bolts. Each bolt sensibly has a nylon washer cushioning the hoop.

■ The batter head bearing edge has a sharp angle of 45°, contributing to the bright sound of the drum. The resonant head bearing edge is the same with no indentation for a snare bed.

■ The tuning bolts require a 0.2in square drum key for tuning and the bolt thread is a standard modern 3/16in–24G.

■ The snare mechanism is a simple throw release and the snares are tensioned with a strip of clear plastic looped through the 50mm wide 20-strand single-course steel wire snares. The snare tension is coarsely adjusted via four drum-key adjustable bolts (two per side) and fine adjustment is via the usual thumbscrew.

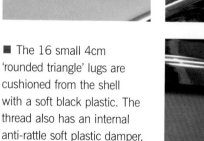

■ The 16 small 4cm 'rounded triangle' lugs are cushioned from the shell with a soft black plastic. The thread also has an internal anti-rattle soft plastic damper, which assists as an anti-detune lock.

■ The six-ply shell is perfectly round and 13.75in diameter, bearing edge to bearing edge.

■ The inner shell is unsupported and the shell thickness is 7.1mm.

■ The vent hole is a lined 9.2mm.

Hardware

The kit comes with a hi-hat, bass-drum pedal, snare and cymbal stands but no cymbals.

■ Bass drum pedal

The PP550 has a reinforced beater holder, chain-screw and rim clamp, plus a single chain, single spring and a ground metal plate for extra stability.

It features an independently adjustable beater angle via a drum key with two options on beater hardness. There are two adjustable anchor spikes to hold the bass drum in place. In a brushed aluminium finish. This is a lot of pedal for little bucks.

■ Cymbal stand

Weight 3kg. The double-braced stand has a substantial tilt mechanism with soft plastic cymbal protectors inbuilt. The range of tilt usefully exceeds 100°.

The memory locks knit neatly into the main oval of the two-stage height-adjustable sections.

■ Hi-hat

Weight (no cymbals) 3kg.

The double-braced tripod has memory locks and a chain-drive.

The lower cymbal has a cushioned cup seating with variable tilt.

The upper cymbal clutch is also cushioned with soft black plastic above and below.

The pedal has a fairly substantial cast metal platform with double spurs.

Unfortunately a design glitch is the plastic cup for the lower cymbal, which arrived broken – this metal to plastic interface perhaps needs more thought. Stagg UK are aware of the problem and immediately dispatched a replacement.

■ Snare stand

Weight 2.75kg. The compact double-braced stand has the same neat memory locks as the cymbal and hi-hat stands, with a substantial locking tilt mechanism and a large 'revolve lever' for the snare basket adjustment.

Bass drum

22in x 16in, weight 10kg.

■ The bass drum's 45mm wooden hoops were protected for travel in strips of the *Guangzhou Daily*. The six-ply appears to be the same as that used for the drum shells.

■ The bearing edge has the same 45° angle as the other drums.

■ As you might expect at this price, the hoops and heads are tensioned with some fairly insubstantial metal claws and utilise the modern approach with square-head tension bolts.

■ Surprisingly the shell thickness is slightly thinner at 6.6mm, and this thin shell has to bear the weight of the mounted toms. The Swiv-O-Matic-type twin tom holder protrudes substantially into the shell cavity.

■ The Swiv-O-Matic-type bearings appear to be ABS plastic secured with a thumb lock. The tom fittings also have memory lock interlocking tenons for a secure fit, and the overall height setting has a more conventional 'ring' memory lock.

■ The bass drum has two substantial 19mm spurs with optional rubber feet or spikes.

■ The 20 lugs are the larger 5cm type as found on the toms.

Tom 1

12in x 10in, weight 3kg. Note the two suspended toms are shell-mounted not RIMS isolated as now found on most more expensive kits (the shell mounting may inhibit the shell resonance – see page 90). These toms have chrome half-hinge type mounts, again isolated from the shell with some soft black plastic, and the clamp is designed to accept a 10mm post.

■ The rims are the same triple-flange pressed steel type as the snare, with six lugs per head. The lugs are 5cm long – slightly larger than the snare but the same soft triangle shape, and the tuning bolts have the standard square head.

■ The shell is, as the snare, 7.1mm thick, perfectly round and the interior unlacquered.

■ Note all the drum fittings – lugs and brackets – were a fraction loose, probably due to shrinkage in transport. It's worth tightening all these before tuning the kit, as inevitably something will rattle!

Tom 2

13in x 11in, weight 3.5kg. This is constructed exactly as tom 1, with six lugs per head.

Tom 3

16in x 16in, weight 6kg.

■ The rims and shells follow the pattern of the two mounted toms with the same 7.1mm shell.

■ The floor tom shares the same shell-mounted tom clamps as the mounted toms but with three clamps securing the 10mm legs, which have rubber feet. The adjustable legs have a form of memory lock with two metal tenons securing these to the shell clamps, conveniently tightened with a standard drum key.

Signed off

No sticks are supplied – which given that every drummer has his own preferences is no great loss. The same applies to cymbals, which need to be individually chosen.

However, the lack of a drum stool may mean some extra expense before the first practice stint. Domestic chairs are rarely the ideal height for drumming.

This is an excellent starter kit that could even be gigged with the addition of some top-of-the-range heads and choice cymbals.

Yamaha Steve Jordan Signature 'Cocktail' kit

Drummers used to travel with all the ease of guitarists and bassists, and a jam in the local bar was possible. This may be the drummer's solution.

Cocktail drums

The 'Carlton King Combination' was a British invention designed for use in cramped orchestra pits in London's West End theatres, and remained in production from 1948 to 1952. The kit consisted of a vertical 20in bass drum, a snare drum, cymbal and other accessory percussion. It was a big hit in one show where the kit featured in *The Indian Love Call*, including timpani pedal-style pitch changes.

Eventually American makers, including Slingerland, Ludwig and Gretsch, began producing cocktail drums. The typical bass drum consisted of a floor tom. The bottom head was struck via a foot-pedal and attuned to achieve a bass-drum sound. The top head was played conventionally with sticks or brushes. The top head also optionally fitted with a snare. The drum's height requires the musician to play standing up, with one foot operating the pedal and the other bearing the musician's weight. This made the drums quite easy to move as a piece! However, the trade-off for this is the practice and balance required to play the instrument. Besides Steve Jordan, other notable players are Pete Erskine, 'Slim Jim' Phantom of the Stray Cats and Paul Beavis of the Andy Fairweather Low band.

Condition on arrival

Supplied by hire company John Henrys this kit has seen a bit of action and needs a good clean; some inconsiderate has left his cocktails all over the heads and shells.

Made in Japan

Getting up and running

I had to think about this one, especially the upside-down bass-drum pedal! However, it soon went together and John Henrys supplied a decent set of Zildjian cymbals, a cowbell and a decent rhythm block. This is not the most stable of kits, as all the hardware hangs off a floor tom, but with a bit of thought given to balance all comes out well.

General description

The main 15in x 24in birch and Philippine mahogany shell combines both bass and snare drums, allowing the drummer to play while standing. An accessory arm accommodates hi-hat, cymbal, cowbell and/or woodblock and has the optional snare and tom as well as a side-mounted Groove-Wedge in Champagne Sparkle – 'shaken not stirred', so not too much brush action.

Steve Jordan

International session drummer Steve Jordan plays Yamaha drums, and together they've developed this useful alternative 'unplugged' kit. As a teenager Steve played for Stevie Wonder, and later he played drums for the *Saturday Night Live* band on US TV. When John Belushi and Dan Aykroyd toured as The Blues Brothers in the early 1980s Jordan became their drummer, and recorded on their first album, credited as Steve 'Getdwa' Jordan. Keith Richards eventually hired Jordan to play on Aretha Franklin's cover of *Jumpin' Jack Flash* for the film of the same name. In the Taylor Hackford documentary *Hail! Hail! Rock'n'Roll*, a tribute to Chuck Berry, he appears in many scenes with Berry and Richards.

Hardware

■ **Bass-drum pedal**
Weight 2.5kg (including fixing bracket).

This reverse action pedal has a single chain-drive, sturdy base plate with grip spurs, and a single spring.

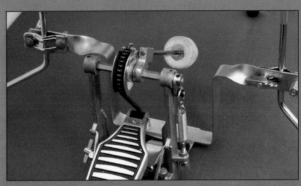

■ **A cymbal and hi-hat 'Budgie' stand**
Attached directly to the bass drum shell with some potential for adjustment.

■ **Cowbell and Meinl 6in and 8in rhythm block**
Both attached to the cymbal stand with accessory clamps.

■ **Cymbals**
The cymbals consist of a Zildjian 10in 'A' hi-hat and a Zildjian 12in 'A' splash. Total weight (including cymbals and accessories) 3.25kg.

The snare

8in x 5in, weight 2kg. Serial number SD08CJ7314. The tiny snare has a Remo 'Weatherking' USA coated batter and a thin clear SD resonant head with five shared lugs per head.

■ The outer 7mm five-ply shell has the Yamaha Steve Jordan signature badge.

■ The snare mechanism is a tiny but well-engineered sprung throw release, and the snares are tensioned with nylon cord through the 14 short high-carbon steel strands. The fine adjustment is via a substantial well-knurled thumbscrew.

■ The five shared lugs are small, body-high tension lugs with isolator and a non-locking nut. All have substantial locking washers secured with a No 1 Phillips.

■ This snare sounds as you'd expect – very high but effective. It's attached to the 'bass drum' via a substantial accessory clamp.

■ The rims are triple-flanged chrome with standard 0.2in tension bolts. The tuning-bolt thread is a standard modern 3/16in–24G.

■ The snare has a slightly rounded 45° bearing edge for both heads.

■ The shell has a substantial snare bed both sides of the resonant rim.

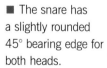

'Bass drum'

15in x 24in, weight 8kg (including side-mounted Groove-Wedge). This is really a very deep tom.

■ The 8.5mm birch and Philippine mahogany shell rings out all the low frequencies to be had at this diameter of head, and has eight individual lugs per head and a diagonal shell joint.

■ The supplied heads are Remo-coated 'Weatherking' Ambassador on the top batter and a double-ply clear pinstripe for the 'bass' batter, both heads being double function. The 45° bearing edge of the batter side of the shell has an additional foam damping ring to suppress high harmonics and thus exaggerate the fundamental 'low' frequencies.

■ The top batter has a fan-style snare that's engaged with a simple adjustable tension bracket, similar to a 1930s style internal damper mechanism.

■ The 'bass drum' also has three substantial and adjustable legs. These are fixed, extend and have optional and non-adjustable rubber feet or spikes.

Tom

5in x 10in, weight 2.25kg. Attached directly to the bass drum with an accessory mount, same as the snare.

■ The six shared lugs are substantial and isolated by soft plastic mounts. The tuning bolts have the standard square head.

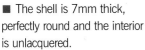

■ The shell is 7mm thick, perfectly round and the interior is unlacquered.

■ The resonant and batter bearing edges are 45°. The heads are a coated Ambassador batter and a clear Ambassador resonant.

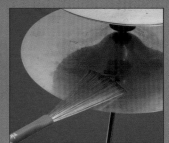

Key players

If we agree that the modern drum set or 'kit' begins with Gene Krupa's Slingerland in the 1930s, then it makes sense that it was the jazz players who propelled that development forward in the '40s. Here the bebop players were important refiners of the instrument – my Dad even referred to his last 1950s Premier set as a 'Bop' kit.

The rock'n'roll explosion of the '50s took up that initiative and developed a solid groove with bass drum, hi-hat and snare, keeping it simple but driving things forward. The drum kit remained essentially identical.

LEFT Let's hear it for the guy at the back who holds the groove. *(Top left and bottom right – Getty Images; bottom left and top right – David Phillips, www.music-images.co.uk)*

RIGHT Where it all began.

The first wave of innovators

In 1935 Gene Krupa didn't just ask Slingerland for some tuneable toms, thereby defining the modern kit: his charisma and verve on the bandstand put the drummer out front, and suddenly everyone recognised 'the man at the back'. When you watch *The Benny Goodman Story* the subtext might easily be the rise of the star drummer.

From here there was no going back, and Jo Jones and Roy Haynes with Charlie Parker, and Max Roach with Dizzy Gillespie became the essential developers of the now ubiquitous ride cymbal style, featuring an increasingly independent and busy left hand decorating the jazz swing. For these guys, often playing small shelled Gretsch kits, toms were a 'frill' – high-tuned and melodic, and that small high-tensioned bass drum was purely for accents. Two cymbals were enough – invariably Zildjian. The calf heads of the era precluded any overt grandstanding – hit them too loud and they simply broke.

BELOW Gene Krupa – the first drum superstar. *(Getty Images)*

ABOVE Art Blakey taking the groove back to Africa. *(Getty Images)*

Art Blakey would eventually take his Gretsch drums back to their African roots with his Jazz Messengers, still leaning on the hi-hat and ride but giving renewed voice to the wider kit. Ed Thigpen playing Remo drums reminded us how versatile and subtle a groove could be had from a virtuosic wire brush.

Connie Kay playing Sonor with the Modern Jazz Quartet remains an underrated innovator, and his use of darbuka, triangle and finger cymbals in the '50s and '60s pre-empted a move to world percussion taken up decades later by Mickey Hart's Planet Drum.

In the 1960s Elvin Jones played Gretsch with Charlie Mingus and John Coltrane, moving jazz into new realms of freedom and self-expression, rolling toms and cymbals into sheets of sound.

Louis Bellson playing Gretsch and Rogers and Eric Delaney with Premier re-invented the extended kit, adding a second bass drum and more toms, a fashion rooted in big band jazz that would much later be adopted by rock. Buddy Rich showed how a four- or five-shell Rogers kit could still drive a huge band and that small splash cymbals could still have a place.

Joe Morello playing Ludwig kits with Dave Brubeck showed us all how musical a drum solo could be – even in

5/4 time. Astonishingly he took that drum
solo *Take Five* into to the pop charts. We're
all still learning the lessons of Joe's subtlety.
Jimmy Cobb on Miles Davis' *Kind of Blue*
showed how less could often be more.

Shelley Manne, equally at home on
vintage Gretsch and revived Leedy drums,
demonstrated the virtue of 'more' with
the Stan Kenton Orchestra.

In the '50s the first rock'n'roll
drummers had taken the 'Bop' kit and
initially struggled with the frailty of calf
heads. 'Chick' Evans and Remo Belli's
mylar would eventually open the door to a
driving back beat and a thunderous bass drum.
Vinyl limitations, however, meant that many early
drum tracks were under-recorded, and many
Buddy Holly and Elvis Presley tracks substitute
cardboard boxes and rhythmically slapped thighs
– easy to record, often very effective, and cheaper
to maintain.

TOP RIGHT Buddy Rich. *(Getty Images)*

RIGHT Louis Bellson. *(Getty Images)*

BELOW Elvin Jones. *(Getty Images)*

Frank Kirkland or Clifton James on *Hey Bo Diddley* took
us away from the simple shuffle, reintroducing toms and
venturing into an Afro-Latin groove. Surf drummer Ron Wilson
with the Surfaris' *Wipeout* brought a paradiddle to number
one on his Sonor kit.

In the 1960s the Motown Funk brothers, with Benny
'Papa Zita' Benjamin, Richard 'Pistol' Allen and Uriel Jones,
told it like it is, developing the perfect pop groove with a
very simple four-drum bitsa kit of Ludwig and Slingerland.
The recorded sound of the kit became more important than
the acoustic sound. In Memphis a similar emphasis was
developed by Stax drummer Al Jackson Jnr – his Gretsch
drums locked to the bass guitar for a hypnotic dance-inducing
series of hits including *Green Onions* and every Wilson Picket
and Otis Redding hit.

A second wave

In the UK the first rock'n'roll drummers included the Shadows' Tony Meehan with a simple four-drum Trixon kit and a tiny but dramatic snare. Solo drums went top ten across the Atlantic divide with Krupa-inspired Sandy Nelson displaying an 'old school' technical proficiency rooted in rudiments with *Let There Be Drums*.

Ringo Starr on Ajax and Premier sets with Rory Storm switched to Ludwig after the second Beatles album. His raw energy came like a bolt from the blue, with no rudiments but a lot of drive. Eschewing any technical limitations, his energy infuses the music with life, and that life conquered the world. As the Beatles developed as musicians Ringo gave an audio lesson to us all in simplicity and taste: 'Serve the song'.

Ringo represents a whole generation of self-taught, totally eccentric and creative drummers of the '60s who often disregarded any conventional technique, substituting a naive creativity worthy of painters like Rousseau. Watching Starr's 'left-handed, right-handed' playing is a revelation in unorthodox solutions. Ringo had no standard technique to fall back on and thus avoids all cliché – he just made something up to fit the song – *Ticket to Ride*, *Rain* and *Come Together* are all bizarre but brilliant.

BELOW John Bonham with a Vistalite Ludwig kit. *(Getty Images)*

ABOVE Ringo Starr with his Premier kit. *(Getty Images)*

Also in England, Bobby Elliot with the Hollies finally got his Premier bass drum heard by employing a wooden beater and a moleskin patch.

Keith Moon startled us all on his Ludwig kit for *Anyway, Anyhow Anywhere*, but the Who soon became synonymous with Red Sparkle Premier and *Pictures of Lily*.

Ginger Baker was rooted in jazz, but his two Ludwig bass-drum thunder on *NSU* and *Toad* from Cream moved the whole idea of rock drummer to a new level.

Mitch Mitchell kept Jimi Hendrix on song playing Premier, Ludwig and astonishing British drums by Hayman.

John Bonham playing Vistalite Ludwig kits moved heavy rock drumming to centre stadium. The recording limitations that gave us the click bass drum and the over-compressed cymbals of the '60s were eventually challenged and Queen's Roger Taylor gave energy to the simplest groove with a huge *We Will Rock You* Ludwig bass drum.

In jazz rock, Tony Williams took drumming to wild new territory, with Miles Davis remaining faithful to his jazz-rooted but expanded Gretsch.

For all of this Zildjian cymbals remained to the fore, with Sabian, Paiste and Istanbul gradually making some headway. Whatever the brand, the ancient Turkish bronze formula remained the sound we all wanted.

After the drum machine anarchy of the mid-'80s Phil Collins heralded the return of the acoustic snare with a huge gated reverb and a flurry of auditorium toms –another Gretsch man.

Dave Mattacks with Paul McCartney had his Yamaha kit shipped out to Air Montserrat, his musicality and careful tensioning ensuring every ounce of groove.

Also on Yamaha, though starting out on Gretsch, Steve Gadd epitomises the notion of 'a musician who happens to play the drums'. Steve's technical virtuosity has always been at the service of the band and the song.

Omar Hakim playing Pearl drove Dire Straits to unprecedented success with *Brothers in Arms*, a digital breakthrough with a startlingly dramatic drum intro from Terry Williams. Hakim would also drive Weather Report and David Bowie. Omar has now associated himself with DW and Roland, though he retains a Pearl signature snare.

In the 1990s Simon Philips challenged all convention with a huge Tama kit behind artists such as Jeff Beck, the Who and Mike Oldfield.

Back in jazz, Billy Cobham startled us all with his eccentric 1970s front-facing shells and is long associated with Meinl cymbals. He now has a long relationship with Yamaha.

Neil Peart with Rush now flies the flag for the extraordinary Rolls Royce drums of DW – drummers have never been better served.

French drummer Manu Katche with Peter Gabriel, Sting, Youssou N'Dour and Dire Straits plays big Yamaha kits to great effect – subtle understated brilliance.

Terry Bozzio takes advantage of DW's Vertical Low Timbre shell technology, wringing every ounce of drive behind Jeff Beck, Frank Zappa and Herbie Hancock.

With limitations of space, I've confined myself to just some of the innovators who moved the groove forward – we are so fortunate now in having *hundreds* of great drummers at the service of global music, so my apologies if I missed your personal favourite. Drums have never been better and the range of cymbals is astonishing, so put down that wrench and count off the band.

TOP RIGHT Steve Gadd. *(Getty Images)*

MIDDLE RIGHT Ginger Baker. *(David Phillips, www.music-images.co.uk)*

RIGHT Neil Peart. *(David Phillips, www.music-images.co.uk)*

DRUM-KIT MANUAL

Appendices, glossary and contacts

My thanks to all the drummers who helped to make this manual happen, especially Steve Street.

LEFT DW tom mount.

RIGHT DW bass drum.

■ Appendix 1
KickPort and resonant head compatibility chart

Head	Notes
Aquarian ported, 4.75in	The hole is too small, and the felt ring must be removed.
Aquarian ported, 7in	The 7in port is too large.
Atta Evans Onyx Resonant	With a 5in port, this head should work fine. The 'control ring' might need to be taped down if it causes noise.
Evans EQ3	With a 5in port, this head should work fine. Remove the 'EQ muffle ring'.
Evans EMAD Resonant	The 5in port will work fine. Remove the foam muffle rings.
Remo Powerstroke 3	With 5in DynamO.
Remo Ambassador (ported)	The 5.5in port is larger than ideal, but should work fine.
Remo Emperor	The two-ply Emperor is one of the demo heads used by FPC. Note that it will need a port cut and reinforcement ring installed.

General criteria a resonant head must meet are:

■ Two-ply heads are preferred, but not necessary.
■ The port must be 5–5.5in in diameter.
■ The port must have a reinforcement ring installed, both to prevent tear-outs and to give the KickPort something to grip.
■ No foam or felt muffling is allowed. This is critical. Heads with built-in foam or felt, such as the Aquarian resonant, must be replaced or stripped of the damping materials.
■ Perimeter rings of head material, as found on the Remo Powerstroke, are acceptable, but these must occasionally be taped down to prevent rattling.
  Source: recordinghacks.com

■ Appendix 2
Useful contacts

eddieryancustomdrums.co.uk
JHS http://www.jhs.co.uk – musical merchandise.
D'Addario UK Ltd, A3 Eleventh Avenue, Gateshead, NE11 0JY – Evans heads.
Vic Firth.com – drumsticks and accessories.
DrumTuna.com.
Regal Tip http://www.regaltip.com – drumsticks.
Vater.com – drumsticks and accessories.
ProtectionRacket.com – cases and bags.
Premier Drum Company, http://www.premier-percussion.com.
DW drums.com, David Philips and John Good.
Yard Gavrilovic – vintagedrumyard.co.uk

■ Appendix 3
Learning resources

Rockschool Drums – graded study books with CD and support materials.
Rhythm Magazine and CD resources.
Drummer Magazine.co.uk.
Vintage Drummer.com.
Modern Drummer sales@halleanard.com.
Not So Modern Drummer.com.
'Lick Library' *Tuning Basics* DVD.

Bass Drum – Usually the largest drum in a kit, played using a pedal-operated beater.

Batter – The head that the drummer plays.

Bearing edge – The point of a drum's shell in contact with the head.

Beater – The pedal-operated hammer used to beat the bass drum.

Bell – The central raised dome of a cymbal.

Bounce – Alternative name for a heavy ride cymbal.

Brushes – Drumsticks that terminate in a fan of thin wires. Used for softer styles of music, most often jazz and ballads.

China cymbal – An 'upside-down' variety of cymbal, in which the edges are turned upwards.

Cocktail drums – Kit in which the bass and snare are combined in a single drum, played standing up. The bottom head is struck by a pedal and the upper head using drumsticks.

Congas – Tapering, long-bodied, hand-beaten drums.

Cowbell – A thick bell akin to those hung round the necks of Alpine cattle.

Crash – A type of cymbal used to produce a loud, crashing accent. Its size varies.

Dampener – Muffling device used to reduce a drum's resonance. Placed either inside the drum or on the head.

Djembe – A waisted, hand drum of African origin.

Drum key or tuning key – A small key used to adjust the tension rods on a drum.

Fill – A variation or drum pattern used as an accent or transition within a tune. Also called a break.

Flares – Flexible wood or plastic drumsticks consisting of a set of adjustable rods also called 'rutes' and 'flix'.

Heads – The upper and lower surfaces of a drum, known as the batter and the resonant respectively. Once commonly made of calfskin vellum, now mylar.

Hi-hat – A pedal-operated pair of cymbals mounted one above the other (the lower one inverted) on a single stand.

Kicked drum or kick – Alternative names for the bass.

Kit – A set of drums.

Lo-hat – Lower-mounted hi-hat. Also known as a 'low boy' or 'sock cymbal'.

Lugs – The metal brackets used to attach a head to a drum.

Mallet – A drumstick with a soft, rounded end, most often for use on cymbals.

O ring or zero ring – A hoop-shaped piece of mylar used to mute a drum's rim harmonics.

Paradiddle – A rudimentary eight-note drum sequence (R L R R L R L L).

Piccolo – A slender variety of snare drum that produces a crisp, tight tone.

Ping – Alternative type of ride cymbal.

Resonant – The head that's not beaten.

Ride – A large, thick cymbal usually played using the tips of the drumsticks.

Rim or hoop – Round head retainer; sits on top of the head and is tightened by means of the tension rods.

RIMS – Resonance isolation mounting system.

Rimshot – Term used to describe tone produced by striking the head and the rim simultaneously.

Shell – The cylindrical, most often wooden outer surface of a drum.

Sizzle – A cymbal in which rivets have been inserted into holes in the disc. Also the sound that such a cymbal makes.

Snare – A set of parallel coiled wires or gut stretched across the lower surface of the drum of the same name.

Snare bed – Indentation in the lower bearing edge of a snare drum.

Splash – A smallish cymbal used to produce a short, high-pitched note.

Spurs – The 'feet' of a bass drum, designed to prevent it from creeping across the floor when it's beaten.

Stack cymbals – Pair of cymbals mounted one above the other on a single stand, or 'stacker'.

Tam-tam – A large gong struck with a soft-headed mallet. Produces a wash of non-specific pitch like a cymbal.

Tension rods or tuners – Screws that tighten the rim to the drum head. Used to adjust the tension of the head.

Throne – Nickname for the drummer's seat or stool.

Throw-off – Release lever that disconnects the snare mechanism from a snare drum, making it sound like a tom.

Timbale – Small, very shallow metal drums that lack a resonant head.

Tom or tom-tom – A drum without a snare. Can be mounted either on the bass drum or on its own stand.

Tone ring – A hoop-shaped piece of mylar used to mute the rim harmonics of a drum.

Toys – Additional percussion instruments sometimes added to a drum kit, such as bells, chimes, rattles etc.

Traps kit – A kit that includes numerous percussion contraptions ('traps') including woodblocks, cowbells, triangles, rattles etc.

Woodblock – Hollowed block of wood played using the drumsticks. Can be of many different shapes and sizes.

Bibliography

DVDs

Steve Gadd, Hudson Music Master Series – hudsonmusic.com
A Tribute to the Legendary Gene Krupa – 'Swing, Swing, Swing!', Hudson Music.
The Duke Ellington Masters 1965 – from the Falcon Theatre Copenhagen, Quantum Leap.
The Duke Ellington Masters 1971 – from Tivoli's Concert Hall Copenhagen, Quantum Leap.

Books

Aldridge, John. *Guide to Vintage Drums* (Centerstream Publishing, 2000).
Cohan, Jon. *Star Sets: Drum Kits of the Great Drummers* (Hal Leonard, 1995).
Cook, Rob. *The Slingerland Book* (Rebeats Publications, 2004).
Hart, Mickey, and Stevens, Jay. *Drumming at the Edge of Magic: A Journey Into the Spirit of Percussion* (Harper San Francisco, 1990).
— and Lieberman, Fredric. *Planet Drum: A Celebration of Percussion and Rhythm* (Harper San Francisco, 1991).
Nicholls, Geoff. *The Drum Handbook: Buying, Maintaining and Getting the Best From Your Drum Kit* (Backbeat Books, 2004).
— *The Drum Book: A History of the Rock Drum Kit* (Backbeat, 2008).
Paiste, Erik. *Paiste Cymbal Guide – Drum Set and Percussion Cymbals* (Paiste, 2010).
Phillips, David. *A Drummer's Perspective* (A. & R. Marketing, 2010).
Pinksterboer, Hugo, and Bierenbroodspot, Gijs. *Tipbook: Drums – The Complete Guide* (Tipbook, 2009).
— and Mattingly, Rick. *The Cymbal Book* (Hal Leonard, 1993).
Schroedl, Scott. *Drum Tuning: The Ultimate Guide* (Hal Leonard, 2002).
— *101 Drum Tips: Stuff all the Pros Know and Use* (Hal Leonard, 2003).
Trynka, Paul (ed.). *Rock Hardware: 40 Years of Rock Instrumentation* (Outline Press, 1999).

Credits

Author – Paul Balmer

Editor – Steve Rendle

Design – Richard Parsons

Copy editor – Ian Heath

Studio photography – John Colley

Technical photography – Paul Balmer

Photo research – Judy Caine

Library photos – Getty Images, David Phillips and National Music Museum, The University of South Dakota

Acknowledgements

My thanks to:

- Steve Gadd for a great interview and the groove on some of my favourite records.
- Yard Gavrilovic – drum tech to the stars, for Steve Gadd kit, Ludwig Downbeat and brilliant advice in general.
- The Vintage DrumYard, Unit 8, Anchor Road Industrial Estate, Clacton-on-sea, Essex CO15 1HP.
- David Brown – vintage drum collector of England, for The Gene Krupa drums.
- Steve Street – drummer, guitarist and all-round good guy, whose fault this book is.
- Colin Tennant and Simon Bramley at Premier Percussion UK for so much help with Premier history and development. They also provided the vintage accessories for the 1960s kit.
- Birmingham Drum Centre www.birminghamdrumcentre.co.uk) – Chris Payne for the DW and Pearl kits and much advice.
- Martin Holland-Lloyd of 'Rattle & Drum' (www.rattleanddrum.com) of Derby, for Tama and accessories.
- Matt Nolan (www.mattnolancustom.com) for great cymbals, triangles and tam-tams.
- Gavin Coulson, JHS artiste liaison manager/national product demonstrator – for many kits and percussion accessories.
- John Good of DW for a fascinating interview and great drums.
- Vater.com Percussion accessories.
- Evans drumheads (www.daddario.co.uk) – Elaine Smith, marketing manager.
- Zildjian Cymbals (www.zildjian.com) – Bob Wiczling and Simon Fraser-Clark at Headstock distribution.
- Protection Racket (www.protectionracket.com) – Dean Bowdery.
- Gavin Thomas and Faye Grigson at Yamaha, for the Steve Gadd and other kits.
- Richard Ashby, marketing and product manager electronic keyboard division, Yamaha Music Europe GmbH (UK) – for electronic kits.
- Gerry Paton – *What Swat: A Guide to Early Wire Brushes* (http://brushbeat.org/documents/What_Swat.pdf).
- Roland V drum experts Hiroyuki Nishi in Japan, and Jonny Carpenter, guitar and drum product manager at Roland (UK) Ltd.
- Andrew Street at Liberty Drums Ltd, 4 Richmond Close, Shildon, County Durham, DL4 1NW (tel 0845 0090672, sales@libertydrums.co.uk).
- Andy McCreeth – for the Matt Nolan pics.
- Smart Ass thrones – Adrian Darby, ADS Drums Percussion Instrument Distribution, and Daniel Darby.
- Dan at Rocky Road Music, Corby, for the drum mikes and great PA.
- Jack Polubinski at www.drumspares.com.
- RecordingHacks.com – KickPort review.
- Properties of Drum Shells and Bearing Edges, Eric J. Macaulay, Department of Physics, University of Illinois at Urbana-Champaign.
- Rob Nathan of Footes Drums, London.
- Connie Kay, Max Roach, Joe Morello, Tony Meehan, Ginger Baker, Keith Moon and Art Blakey for showing the way.

Index